THE MODERN BRITISH MONARCHY

THE MODERN BRITISH MONARCHY

J. A. THOMPSON / ARTHUR MEJIA, JR.

ST. MARTIN'S PRESS
NEW YORK

AFFILIATED PUBLISHERS: Macmillan & Company, Limited, London—also at Bombay,
Calcutta, Madras and Melbourne; The Macmillan Company of Canada, Limited, Toronto.

PREFACE

The survival of the British monarchy strikes many observers as an anomaly. In an age when the virtues of democracy, equality, and representative institutions are seen as the highest expressions of political wisdom, monarchy appears strikingly out of place. It is, after all, a matter of tradition and inherited privilege; it rests on a set of presumptions about sovereignty and human behavior that are impressively different from those which are supposedly the basis of our modern conception of government. Yet the British monarchy has managed to survive, and has adapted itself successfully to the twentieth century. To a great extent, this adaptation has been accidental, but a study of the circumstances involved can throw considerable light on recent British history and on the political, psychological, and sociological pressures of the modern world. A study of the changes in the British monarchy over the last century and a half, therefore, entails far more than an analysis of the evolution of a "declining" institution; it involves an analysis of many of the important aspects of political and social behavior.

It is necessary, from the outset, to stress the fact that the British monarchy is an important institution. The Queen is a figurehead, but she is also much more. She is a formidable person who plays a far larger role in the life of the nation than many historians and social scientists admit. The significance of the monarchy is often underestimated because it is taken for granted. Not infrequently this is the case with the British themselves. But were royalty to disappear everyone would be conscious of the change, not only because of the significant constitutional complications that would ensue, but also because of the resulting social and emotional ramifications. National loyalty would have to find different and probably less beneficial outlets; fundamental changes would take place in the role of politics in the life of the nation as a whole; and there would be profound shifts in the public attitude toward deference to tradition and hierarchy. Should the monarchy ever disappear, such changes would of course already have taken place. It has survived, often not so much because of its own strength as because it has filled so well the needs of a "paternalistic" society. It does have, however, strengths of its own, for it reflects and incorporates many of the desires felt by all modern societies, especially the need for the personalization of government. The monarchy, that is, has helped many persons to overcome the terrible anonymity and alienation of modern life.

This book will trace the development of the monarchy from the early nineteenth century to the present, explaining how each stage of its evolution contributed to its ability to meet the needs of an urban, industrial, and increasingly democratic nation. It will discuss the *mystique* of modern kingship, and will explain how a seemingly anachronistic institution came to play a vital role, politically, sociologically, and psychologically, in contemporary Britain.

CONTENTS

CHAPTER 1

THE VICTORIAN MONARCHY

Queen Victoria and Prince Albert were the founders of the modern British monarchy, one of the most accidentally successful political institutions of recent times. Yet in 1837, when the Queen ascended the throne, the outlook for that institution was most unpromising. For a generation the dynasty had been represented principally by the unattractive children of George III, especially by the Prince Regent, who became George IV in 1820, and by a younger son, William IV. Except for the just fame of the Regent as a patron of the decorative arts, these children had little to recommend them. Their personal lives had been unwholesome by just about any standard; to put it as tactfully as possible, they did not fulfill the criteria which nineteenth-century Englishmen had come to expect in their royalty. They continued, moreover, to cling to an interpretation of the royal prerogative which, though it was not generally considered outdated at the time, could scarcely have survived the next few decades. Although there was virtually no republican movement in England in the 1830s, many Englishmen suspected that the Hanoverian family would fall from the throne by the weight of its own incompetence; in that event England, the most "advanced" of European countries, might well become a republic, *faute de mieux.*

The succession to the throne of the attractive, vivacious, eighteen-year-old Princess Victoria admittedly gave the monarchy a breathing spell; the contrast between the new Queen and her dissolute uncles was so startling that one could not help being charmed. The change in 1837, however, was only superficial. If Victoria's tendencies toward sexual license had been well controlled by a careful upbringing, she was nevertheless completely Hanoverian in her stubborn determination to have her own way in everything; whether the issue was frivolous or serious, the Queen was convinced that her position gave her the right to prevail. In fact, the throne freed her from the severely restricted life to which her mother had subjected her at Kensington Palace, and she was determined to make the most of it.[1]

In 1837 the concept of a constitutional monarchy, as we use that term today, had not developed. It was assumed that the sovereign would play an important and partisan role in politics, and would have a specific policy which he would endeavor to implement. Certainly this was the case with William IV: "In his short reign of seven years, he twice dismissed a Ministry; twice dissolved Parliament for political purposes before its time; three times made formal proposals to his Ministers for a coalition with their political opponents; and on one celebrated occasion allowed his name to be used, independently of his political advisers, to influence a crucial vote in the House of Lords."[2] In fact, King William was far more energetic than his older brother in exercising the royal prerogatives, which he did not hesitate to use to further his own political views. His most dramatic act was the dismissal of the Whig ministry in 1834, primarily because of his disapproval of Lord John Russell's plan to appropriate the funds of the Irish Church. The prime minister, Lord Melbourne, proposed to make Russell Leader of the House and Chancellor of the Exchequer; this would have greatly increased Lord John's chances of carrying out his policy. As far as the King was concerned, the obvious course for him to follow was to dismiss the ministry, which he proceeded to do.

Although no one suspected it at the time, this was the last dismissal of a Ministry by the Crown; Sir Robert Peel, who succeeded Melbourne, resigned when it became clear that a majority of the House of Commons was against him, and, after some squirming, William IV recalled Melbourne on April 11, 1835. This, in retrospect, made it clear that the King was helpless if he did not have an alternative ministry that could command the support of the House of Commons. The King was, therefore, humiliated; even when he told Melbourne that, because of the Coronation Oath, his conscience would make it impossible for him to assent to the Irish Church Bill, Melbourne made it clear that the King would have to accept his Ministry's advice, conscience or no conscience, or try to get another government.

But it must be emphasized that no one argued that the King had acted unconstitutionally; he might have acted unwisely or stupidly, but he was within his rights in dismissing a Ministry. Queen Victoria, accordingly, had good reason to think that she might have her way; the precedent set on April 11, 1835 was not yet clear. Furthermore, the situation in the House of Commons after 1837 gave the throne greater latitude for action than had been the case before because, in the election that followed Victoria's accession, the Whigs lost most of their majority. The Queen, therefore, used her position to support her political allies, who were the Whigs. It was considered perfectly acceptable that a party should profit from the favor of the sovereign, and Melbourne certainly thought that turnabout was fair play after the partiality which William IV had shown to the Tories. The Queen became, moreover, passionately attached to Melbourne, and could not envision without horror his removal from office.

All this culminated in the rather ridiculous "Bedchamber Crisis" of 1839. Upon the resignation of the Whig ministry Victoria sent reluctantly for Peel who, because of the well-known partisanship of the Queen for the Whigs, asked, as a gesture of royal confidence, that some of the Whig ladies at court be replaced. The Queen refused, and as a result Peel did not form a government. Admittedly his position was not strong, as he did not have a majority in the Commons, but this "crisis" shows clearly that royal favor was still considered of some importance in the formation of a ministry. When the Queen conspicuously refused to show her confidence in Peel it contributed to Melbourne's return to office. Victoria succeeded in 1839 where her uncle had failed in 1835 because she did have an alternate ministry.

But if the old interpretation of royal power survived into Victoria's reign, it did not survive for long. The Queen, in her youth, did not have a consistent policy, but only passionate attachments. She did not see the Whigs so much as a political party—if such a word is appropriate for the first half of the nineteenth century—but as an extension of Lord Melbourne. If the Whigs went, he went, and that she could not tolerate. Yet, if the affections of the passionate Hanoverian Queen found a new object, her views could change dramatically. This is exactly what happened in 1840 with her marriage to her first cousin, Albert of Saxe-Coburg-Gotha; Albert was her new Melbourne, who "had his own view of the raffish atmosphere of favorites and partisans, both personal and political, in which Victoria moved with every appearance of satisfaction; . . . all he learned of the preceding events of the reign hardened his determination to make a fundamental change in the political role of the monarchy."[3] So the monarchy changed with the coming of the Albertine period; it remained actively involved in politics, but became nonpartisan. It is inconceivable that Victoria, without Albert's influence, could have accepted, even to the limited extent she did, the "conception of a supra-party constitutional monarchy," which traded direct power for influence, and which replaced obstruction with mediation. Had it not been for the influence of the Prince, the Queen would undoubtedly have continued to play a political game which would eventually have brought disaster to the throne; Albert set the course which made possible the development of the modern monarchy.

None of this means, of course, that the history of the Victoria's reign was henceforth one of bland political neutrality. Clearly her personality, which was anything but bland, rendered such a contingency most unlikely. She never hesitated to express her feelings and thoughts in the most direct manner; at times she would use extraordinary wiles and guiles to get her way, as Lord Palmerston, to give but one example, learned on many occasions. Moreover, the opportunities open to Victoria for the exercise of influence were varied and, to a considerable extent, remain in operation today.

Primarily, Victoria could combine the prestige of her office most effectively with the accumulated knowledge of many years, and, eventually, of many decades. This knowledge she built up by a devotion to duty which cannot fail to impress. She saw herself as the center of the British government; no matter where she was, no matter how distracted she might be, the work of government continued. To her this meant the endless reading of state papers, and the frequent cross-examining of ministers and officials of all kind. For someone with the time and inclination few things are more revealing than reading the Queen's published letters. G. E. Buckle was quite right when he wrote in the introduction to one of the volumes of these letters: "Nothing will strike the reader of these pages more than the diligent care with which her Majesty applied herself, day after day, to her duties as a Constitutional Monarch. . . . As a result of this vigilant and assiduous attention to public business, she exercised throughout her reign a very real influence on the course of affairs at home and abroad, especially in times of crisis. . . ."[5] The minister in attendance often found his life difficult, and the questions and the complaints of the Queen were always a matter of concern to a government, if for no other reason than the time involved in answering them.

The Queen, accordingly, interpreted her role as a "constitutional" monarch in a way quite different from today's. She did not see herself merely as a cipher acting only on instructions from her ministers; as far as she was concerned, the expression *her* ministers was no polite legal and constitutional fiction, but the affirmation of reality. There is no doubt that "the divine right of Kings" was not dead as far as she was concerned, for, as was written at her death, in her

> own heart . . . [she] never questioned that she was the anointed of the Lord, called by the most solemn warrant to rule a great nation in the fear of God. . . . When the Queen spoke of her subjects as 'loyal,' she meant it in the mediaeval sense. The relation was not, in her eyes, voluntary or sentimental, but imperative. If she had been a wicked or a foolish woman, it would have been very sad, but the duty of obedience would, in her idea, have been the same. Subjects must be 'loyal'; if they loved their sovereign, so much the better for them and for her, but affection was not essential.[6]

The "Albertine" interpretation of the role of the monarchy, therefore, was never fully grasped by the Queen, for during her reign she frequently violated its basic tenet, political neutrality. Of course, Albert himself, in common with most of the politicians of the day, would not have interpreted neutrality as strictly as his descendants must today, but it is doubtful if he would have approved of the Queen becoming so conspicuously partisan so often and thus weakening, to at least some extent, the influence she might have had. Together with her isolation—something which will be discussed shortly—this partisanship prevented the development of close and friendly relations with all her ministers; her influence, in short, "was dissipated in reprimands and injunctions, often shrewd, always vigorous, but sometimes petulant and sometimes petty."[7] The greatest example of this partisanship is her well-known attachment to Disraeli, and her overpowering loathing of Gladstone. Fortunately for the future of the throne Gladstone believed devoutly in the institution of monarchy and this faith was never weakened by countless snubs, both political and personal. Disraeli, unlike his rival, knew exactly how to handle the Queen, and his success was so great that all Victoria's Hanoverian passion sprang forth to support her devotion to him. But it is important to remember, as Robert

Blake points out, that the Queen disliked Gladstone not just because he treated her as the embodiment of an institution rather than as a woman, but primarily because she disliked and distrusted his policies; Victoria never considered hiding that dislike and distrust in the interest of monarchical neutrality. The Queen, as her letters show, was a convinced Conservative Imperialist and worked to further her views; she was not content to act as a mediator who might exercise subtle and indirect influence.[8]

Nevertheless, Albert's influence avoided what probably would have been highly dangerous situations for the monarchy, and after his death the growth of the party system and the gradual democratization of the suffrage so limited the Crown's opportunities for direct interference that Victoria was shielded from the consequences of her temperament. But it is interesting to speculate on the course of events had Albert not died at the age of forty-two in 1861. Disraeli's *bon mot*—had Albert lived, "he would have given us, while retaining our constitutional liberties, the blessings of absolute government"—can only be taken as a compliment, for it indicated that Albert was recognized as an extremely able man. As Lytton Strachey wrote:

> Already at the time of his death he filled a unique place in English political life; already among the inner circle of politicians he was accepted as a necessary and useful part of the mechanism of state. . . . And, as time went on, the Prince's influence must have enormously increased. For, in addition to his intellectual and moral qualities, he enjoyed, by virtue of his position, one supreme advantage which every other holder of high office was without: he was permanent. Politicians came and went, but the Prince was perpetually installed at the centre of affairs. Who can doubt that, towards the end of the century, such a man, grown grey in the service of the nation, virtuous, intelligent, and with the unexampled experience of a whole lifetime of government, would have acquired an extraordinary prestige.[9]

The Prince Consort, in other words, would have developed the full potentialities of the constitutional monarchy much more ably than his widow. This view obviously assumes a tolerance and a flexibility that Albert might not have possessed.[10]

Any discussion of the influence of the monarchy must necessarily be vague, for the essence of that influence is in its subtlety. Walter Bagehot, in 1867, wrote of the rights of the sovereign: the right to be consulted, the right to encourage, and the right to warn; clearly these rights are exercised effectively only in private. Whether the sovereign's advice carries any weight at all depends on its being confidential; it can be rejected, or accepted, without anyone's prestige becoming involved. A minister can listen with as many or as few reservations as he may choose; the Queen can talk with no fear of public rebuke or humiliation. The confidential nature of the relationship between the Queen and her ministers allows, furthermore, for a personal rapport to develop which can be of the greatest assistance to the sovereign in the tactful application of influence. As mentioned above, this is where Victoria can be faulted, for her political passions made it impossible for her to develop friendly relations with many of her ministers. For the historian, however, the necessary subtlety and secrecy of royal influence makes it difficult to discuss with any degree of precision. It is usually only after the death of a sovereign that much of interest and importance is revealed, and even then what is revealed is unquestionably only a small part of what actually happened, for the consultation, the encouragement, and the warnings take place, as a general rule, in such a way as to avoid their future discovery in the Royal Archives. It is also extremely difficult to chart the rise, or the fall, of the power or the influence of the monarchy: just what the power and influence may be will vary from time to time, depending upon the political situation of the moment and the personalities involved. To some extent such imprecision is found in all governmental systems, but the British "constitution" makes the imprecision far greater because of its dependence upon precedence, unspoken understandings, and the customs of a governing elite in a small nation.

Victoria's views all proceeded from the basic assumption that the institutions of England were fundamentally sound: they had been responsible for England's rise to greatness. Any threat to those institutions was dangerous for the country, and, therefore, a threat to her own position.

The Queen was, therefore, particularly shrill in her objections when she feared some alteration in the structure of the state. She was, as one would certainly suspect, horrified by any threat to the House of Lords. She wrote to Lord Rosebery in 1894 that "The House of Lords might possibly be improved, but it is *part* and *parcel* of the *much vaunted* and *admired British Constitution,* and CANNOT be *abolished.* It is the ONLY REALLY independent House, for it is not bound as the House of Commons is, where they are constantly made to say what they would not otherwise do by their constituents, whom they try to please in order to be elected."[11] Or, as she wrote to W. E. Forster in 1884, "No one can be more *truly* liberal at heart than the Queen is, but she also thinks, that the great *principles* of the *Constitution* of this *great country* ought to be maintained and preserved, and that too many alterations and changes (and there have been so many) should be avoided."[12] In 1880, in another letter to Forster, she put her views very bluntly: the Queen "*cannot* and will not be the Queen of a *democratic monarchy.*"[13]

Her prejudices were very much the same in matters dealing more broadly with the structure of society. Education, for example, was being carried too far, and "ruined the health of the higher classes uselessly, and rendered the working classes unfitted for good servants and labourers."[14] The agitation for woman's rights was even more frightening to Victoria; she thought the movement "dangerous and unchristian and unnatural."

> The Queen is a woman herself — & knows what an anomaly her *own* position is. . . . But to tear away all the barriers w[h] surround a women, & to propose that they sh[ld] study with *men* — things w[h] c[ld] not be named before them — certainly not in a mixed audience — w[ld] be to in-

troduce a total disregard of what must be considered as belonging to the rules & principles of morality. Let woman be what God intended; a helpmate for a man — but with totally different duties and vocations.[15]

As she wrote to Sir Theodore Martin in 1870:

> The Queen is most anxious to enlist every one who can speak or write to join in checking this mad, wicked folly of "Woman's Rights", with all its attendant horrors, on which her poor feeble sex is bent, forgetting every sense of womanly feeling and propriety. . . .
> It is a subject which makes the Queen so furious that she cannot contain herself. God created men and women different—then let them remain each in their own position. . . . Woman would become the most hateful, heathen, and disgusting of human beings were she to unsex herself. . . .[16]

The Queen, incidentally, had both an extremely snobbish and an extremely antisnobbish streak. For example, although she disliked much of the upper class, she reacted unfavorably to the elevation of W. H. Smith to post of first lord of the Admiralty: "It may *not please* the navy in which so many of the *highest rank* serve. . . . if a man of the Middle Class is placed above them. . . ."[17] Of course, the Queen was also simply being realistic. On the other hand, she sent farsighted and humane advice in 1898 to the new Viceroy of India, George Curzon, in which she warned against "the *snobbish* and vulgar, over-bearing and offensive behaviour" of many British officials, and urged greater attention to native feeling.[18] Victoria had great affection for her Indian subjects and servants.

Although the Queen's opinions concerned her ministers, for they had to be answered, they are not really indicative of the influence which she was able to exercise in politics. As Frank Hardie has aptly put it, "The Queen, with the aid of a Private Secretary and virtually no one else, made herself one of the great Departments of State."[19] Clearly she exercised some influence over political appointments, although the pressures she brought to bear were generally intended to block the careers of men like Bradlaugh, Dilke, and Labouchere, all of whom she considered immoral and revolutionary monsters.[20] If in 1880 she could not prevent Gladstone from becoming Prime Minister, in 1894 she refused to consult him regarding his successor, and sent for Rosebery, who probably would not have been recommended by the retiring Prime Minister, although he was apparently the choice of the majority of the Liberal leaders. During Disraeli's second administration she played an important role in securing passage of the Royal Titles Act of 1876, which made her Empress of India, and of a bill to regulate vivisection.[21] In matters dealing with the army she also played an active and highly reactionary role, opposing virtually all change and supporting her cousin, the Duke of Cambridge who, for thirty-nine years, was commander in chief.[22] But more important examples of the Queen's reference can be found in other fields.

In foreign affairs Victoria regarded herself as being of particular importance. She was especially eager that the conduct of her foreign relations be in the hands of the right sort of people, and, at the end of her reign, she had the pleasure of dealing with Lord Salisbury, both as Prime Minister and Foreign Secretary. He was a man with whom she shared a great many views. The harmony between them, and the deference which Salisbury showed to the Crown must not, of course, make one forget that in foreign affairs as well as in domestic affairs royal power declined sharply during the nineteenth century. Nevertheless, Victoria saw foreign affairs as essentially a family matter,* and thus followed them with a passion that was far more personal than political. As Salisbury's daughter wrote, "Drawing her facts from her large private correspondence, illuminated by old experience, she would discuss the characters and motives of the sovereigns and statesmen of Europe much in the same way that an intelligent and observant county gentleman's wife might discuss those of her county neighbors."[23] The best illustration of this is shown in her attitude to her first grandchild, William II of Germany. As far as she was concerned, he was a member of her family first, and the Kaiser second. In 1888, for example, she reacted with fury when she learned that William had been angered by an allegedly casual attitude on the part of the Prince of Wales

> ... as regarding the Prince's not treating his nephew as Emperor; this is really too *vulgar* and too absurd, as well as untrue, almost *to be believed*.
>
> We have always been very intimate with our grandson and nephew, and to pretend that he is to be treated *in private* as well as in public as "his Imperial Majesty" is *perfect madness*! He has been treated just as we should have treated his beloved father and even grandfather, and as the Queen *herself* was always treated by her dear uncle King Leopold. *If* he has *such* notions, he [had] better *never* come *here*.

It is clear that to Victoria the kingdoms of Europe were the estates of various members of her family, and that she hardly distinguished her personal connections with her relatives from the foreign policy of Great Britain. In short, for her "nothing was more natural than the blend of family fetishism with sovereign dignity."[25]

The Foreign Office was certainly conscious of its relationship to the Queen. Everything sent to her "had to be written in a special ink, dried carefully near the fire to bring out the colour of the ink and then blotted with sand."[26] Salisbury himself wrote to the Queen after each Cabinet meeting, as well as at the end of the day when the afternoon's interviews were over. Admittedly he did not send Victoria all incoming despatches and drafts of all outgoing instructions; in practice he selected those papers which he thought she should read, and many handwritten despatches marked "Draft" were in fact copies of letters already sent.[27] Neverthe-

---

*With good reason; see Appendix E.

less, "although the Queen's judgements were often impulsive and emotional, Salisbury did not disregard her advice. Time and experience had
sharpened her wits and the Prime Minister found that her views often
gave him 'an indication of the thought and feelings of the great mass of the
English people.'"[28] Lady Salisbury was sure that the Prime Minister told
the Queen everything,[29] and there were certainly times when the Queen's
influence over her grandson the Kaiser was extremely valuable, as the
Prime Minister was quite willing to admit.[30] Thus it is clear that at the end
of a long reign Victoria was a significant and time-consuming factor in British foreign affairs. When Salisbury was asked how he bore the strain of
holding two offices, he replied: "As for that, I could do very well with two
departments; in fact, I have four,—the Prime Ministership, the Foreign Office, the Queen, and Randolph Churchill,—and the burden of them
increases in that order."[31]

Another area in which the Queen exercised considerable influence was
in church affairs. She was a fanatic supporter of Protestantism, and was
inclined to see popery as an ever-present threat: In 1869 she wrote to
Lord Granville that "The Gov't. and many people in this country seem to
the Queen to be totally blind to the alarming encroachments and increase
of the R. Catholics in England and indeed all over the world. The Pope
was never so powerful. . . . Every favour granted to the R. Catholics does
not conciliate them, but leads them to be more and more grasping and
encroaching and the danger of this to Protestant England cannot be over-
rated."[32] It is not surprising, therefore, that the Queen, as Owen Chadwick
remarks, had a sense of responsibility for the welfare of the church, was
impressively well-informed about its activities and personalities, and
tenaciously defended her right to appoint its leaders.[33] The Queen realized
that, as a rule, the prime minister must initiate nominations, and that she
could only suggest names for general consideration, but the older she
became the more vigorously she would oppose the appointment of those
of whom she disapproved, and "an ignorant prime minister found that the
Queen was better informed than he, and speedily diminished his ignorance
if he wanted to carry his point." Victoria was "a kind of jury, of perfect integrity and unpalatable frankness," before whom prime ministers were
forced to justify their nominations.[34] Disraeli, for one, was scarcely in a
position to do so, for, as he admitted in 1868, "I don't know the names
and descriptions of the persons I am recommending for deaneries and
mitres;" at Balmoral, where, as he once remarked, "Ecclesiastical affairs
rage," he was obviously at a disadvantage.[35] In the appointment of
Archibald Tait to the Archbishopric of Canterbury in 1868 the Queen's
will was decisive; she played a central role in the passage of the Public
Worship Regulations Act of 1874; far more important, however, was the
general and long-term impact of the Queen on ecclesiastical affairs. Partly
because of her influence the idea of choosing a bishop for political reasons
became disreputable, and her desire for moderate men of high standing
helped to produce "a bench of bishops more eminent in wisdom, learning,
personality and holiness of life, than the Church of England had hitherto
seen."[36] Important as the affairs of the Church of England were in the

nineteenth century, it is obviously true that they were not at the center of politics; this enabled the Queen to exercise greater influence than she was able to in more vital areas. If this illustrates the decline of royal power it also shows the opportunities that are available to the intelligent and strong-willed sovereign for effective intervention in issues which are of marginal concern to politicians but which, in the long run, may still influence the nation's history.

Important as the Queen may have been in the political affairs of Great Britain, she was of far greater importance in transforming the monarchy into a symbol of national unity; this, to a great extent, became possible only as the obvious political power of the Crown declined. By her death

> The great Queen, who was grandmother to half the ruling houses of Europe, had become, by virtue of her very age, both a national and an international institution. It was difficult to conceive of either Britain or Europe without the Queen of England, and though Britain's policy of "Splendid Isolation" and her *Superbia Britannorum* might enrage the governments and peoples of the Continent, their dislike of Britain was held in check by their involuntary veneration of that country's tremendous sovereign.[37]

At home it became increasingly difficult, by the end of her reign, to separate loyalty to the nation from loyalty to the Queen. Victoria came to possess "an inspired genius for familiarising virtues," and a "sympathy and sanity [which] made [the English] feel at home even in an age of revolutions;" in short, she appealed to the Englishman's sense of security; she was "so thoroughly English." She may not have relinquished "the whole of that political and legal department of life which is concerned with coercion, regimentation and punishment," but in some strange way she did become "the symbol of the sweeter and purer relation of humanity."[38]

Much of the Queen's success resulted from the fact that she embodied many of the virtues which the middle class came to admire: she was diligent, moral, and thrifty. Moreover, she stood for the sanctity of the family. She might have been the supreme symbol of the greatest Empire in history, but she was also a mother whose concern with her family was the basis of her life. It is doubtful if she could have been such a national and imperial symbol if she had not, with the help of longevity, first come to represent all the virtues of the basic unity in society, the family. For all her concern with foreign affairs, for all her desire to have her children well married, Victoria was obsessed with the happiness of all her descendants. To an extent which would have been surprising only a few decades before, Victoria, like many of her fellow monarchs, "had exchanged the traditional purposes of hereditary monarchs—power and glory—for the dream of subjects: happy domesticity."[39] None of this means, of course, that the British royal family had a "happy" life in the contemporary sense, but it does mean that the sovereign became identified with his or her family as well as with the nation.

But the Victoria of the Jubilees of 1887 and 1897 was a long time in developing. Even if the early part of her reign is disregarded, a period when, because of youth and inexperience, she often incurred considerable unpopularity, it is striking that her emergence as the sacred embodiment of the nation and empire did not occur until relatively late in her reign. The best example of this is the "republican movement" of the late 1860s and the early 1870s. How deep this republicanism went is hard to say; certainly it was intellectually respectable and had the advantage which always attaches to slightly shocking causes. It benefited from the fact that England was in the midst of an age of experiment, reform, and social change. Furthermore, there seems little doubt that the Franco-Prussian War and the fall of the Second French Empire in 1870 played a significant part in the enthusiasm for republicanism. But far more important was the Queen's isolation from her people. Ignoring the demand for public appearances, and retiring within her tight little world of Windsor-Balmoral-Osborne, she showed no sense of what today would be called public relations. Obsessed with grief over her husband's death, and fortified by her conviction that her position in the state was beyond any legitimate criticism, she failed to understand that "industry in private" was not enough to compensate for nonappearance in public; even when she promised to appear she often reneged at the last minute, particularly if she disapproved of the current government.

The rapid decline in royal popularity greatly worried Gladstone,[40] and in 1871 Disraeli felt obliged to counter antimonarchical propaganda in a speech at Hughenden:

> A very erroneous impression is prevalent respecting the duties of the Sovereign in this country. Those duties are multifarious; they are weighty, and they are increasing. I will venture to say that no head of any department in the State performs more laborious duties than fall to the Sovereign of this country. There is not a despatch received from abroad nor one sent from this country which is not submitted to the Queen. The whole internal administration of the country greatly depends upon the sign manual; and of our present Sovereign it may be said that her signature has never been placed to any public document of which she did not know the purport and of which she did not approve.[41]

One wonders if the Queen was really flattered by the last sentence.

The concern of Gladstone and Disraeli was not unjustified. Some important public figures were being drawn toward republicanism—for example Joseph Chamberlain and Charles Dilke. Chamberlain, speaking at the Birmingham Town Hall in September 1870, at a meeting held to express sympathy with the new French Republic, said that he did "not feel any great horror at the idea . . . of the possible establishment of a Republic in this country." Interrupted by cheers, he went on to say that he was "quite certain that sooner or later it will come."[42] Admittedly this republicanism of Chamberlain's may have been mostly intellectual speculation, for he then said that "there is really not any great political difference between a free constitutional monarchy such as ours and a free republic;"[43] nevertheless, Chamberlain did write to Dilke in the fall of 1871 that a republic "at the rate at which we are moving . . . will come in our generation."[44] Dilke, who often spoke at republican rallies, was doing his best to make this prediction come true.

The bitterness of many Englishmen at the Queen's seclusion had been building up for many years, and was being freely expressed.[45] Late in 1871 the *Times* was strongly critical:

> We have frequently and forcibly expressed regret that *Her Majesty* should not feel equal to discharge the duties of hospitality which the nation expects of her, and should occasionally retire to Balmoral or Osborne when her presence is most needed in or near London.[46]

Moreover, the issue of Prince Arthur's allowance had provided the opportunity for strong attacks in the House of Commons. The Radical Peter Alfred Taylor of Leicester said on July 31, 1871:

> There are two special grounds on which I oppose this grant. The first is, that the people ought not to be taxed for services not rendered; and the second is that if it be essential such provision be made, the people have already made sufficient provision.[47]

On the same day the Birmingham Liberal, George Dixon, was even more explicit in his opposition:

> The cessation of the discharge of what may be called Her Majesty's duties, while resulting in no disadvantage to the country politically, ought to have led to a corresponding saving which might have been effected for the maintenance of other members of the Royal Family. I will not deny that there is among the working people a large amount of Republicanism; I know that such a feeling does exist, and that it is increasing. But I think that Republican feeling is of the vaguest possible kind. . . . But there is one feature in their mind, and it is that, rightly or wrongly, they consider that Republican institutions would be less costly than monarchy.[48]

The financial issue was also the subject of the famous pamphlet, published in 1871, *What Does She Do With It?* Once again the excuse for attack was the proposed annuity for Prince Arthur. It was alleged that "There is not a lady in Christendom better able out of her own resources, to provide for every one of her family than our Queen." The Queen, by not maintaining a Court on the same scale as her predecessors, had been able to save large amounts of money; and so, it was implied, why was it necessary to make further provision?[49]

The attack on the monarchical principle often took on a highly personal note. Charles Bradlaugh, who espoused atheism, birth control, woman's suffrage, and compulsory education as well as republicanism, turned his talent for invective on an inviting target, the Prince of Wales. In an address given in the autumn of 1871 to the London Republican club he said:

> Many of you are aware that I have lately and repeatedly declared my most earnest desire that the present Prince of Wales should never dishonour this country by becoming its King. My opinion is that if four or five years of political education are allowed to continue in this land, that worthy representative of an unworthy race will never be King of England. My thorough conviction is that neither his intelligence, nor his virtues, nor his political ability, nor his military capacity—great as all these are for a member of his family—can entitle him to occupy the throne of Great Britain. I am equally opposed to his ever being Regent of England. I trust that he may never sit on the throne or lounge under its shadow.[50]

Moreover, in his pamphlet, *The Impeachment of the House of Brunswick*, first published in 1871, Bradlaugh infuriated many English by characterizing George I and his successors as useless foreigners whom Englishmen paid to "perpetuate a pauper prince race." Bradlaugh, however, was not alone in leveling personal attacks on the Prince, whose private life (to be discussed in the next chapter), did upset many English, including Victoria herself. It must be admitted, furthermore, that Bradlaugh's attacks did not stem entirely from a personal distaste for royalty in general and Hanoverians in particular, but also from a deep feeling that progress of all types was being thwarted by the survival of the monarchy; with a republic would come fraternity, humanity, and a setting condusive to happiness. No violence would be necessary, for on the Queen's death Parliament would simply deny the throne to her heir, and declare a republic; an educated population would see clearly the desirability of such an act.[51]

The year 1871 was, accordingly, not a good one for the monarchy. Republican clubs sprang up all over the country. In April the government allowed a republican demonstration in Hyde Park. In 1872, however, the attack on the monarchy reached its highest point intellectually, with an impressive denunciation by the lawyer and positivist Frederick Harrison. He attacked the monarchy for being, socially, "the consecration of the present," and said that it had no political importance. Furthermore, the

> high attribute of monarchy to elevate the vulgar to the adoration of wealth ought not to blind responsible persons to facts. . . . There is a very wide and deep republican feeling more or less definite and conscious. In London and the great cities the bulk of the working-classes are republican by conviction, unless they are perfectly indifferent. . . . [In the] body of the smaller shopkeeping class, loyalty to the throne finds its highest expression in royal footmen and portraits of a princess; nor is it more likely to take a more solid form. The heir to the Crown is "popular," but he is just as popular in the United States, where huzzaing a notability can hardly be mistaken for politi-

cal principle. And popularity is a vague term. . . . In Ireland they are raising a statue to a beloved greyhound. . . . The obstinate worship of a dead form may seriously hamper growth. . . . England is amongst the first of the nations simply because it is in essence republican— because it has long passed into that stage in which public opinion is the foundation of power, and capacity its true qualification—because it has long passed out of that stage in which allegiance is an accident of birth, and government a piece of property. England is, in heart, republican, because it has asserted in all material things, past question and past change, the principle that the public good is the sole standard, and personal fitness the real criterion of civil power. . . . As the ceremonial Majesty of the throne grows daily more alien to all our self-respect, the practical Majesty of the nation becomes a more present force.[52]

By 1875 the attack on the monarchy was no longer being sustained on such a high level, but in September of that year Bradlaugh's *National Reformer* did publish a poem called the "English Marseillaise":

> Has England forgotten Cromwell's teaching?
> Is Hampden's poured-out blood all in vain?
> Shall the land which saw a King's impeaching
> Now be bound by a Brunswick chain?
> Our sires veil their faces in shame
> For the sons who disgrace their name,
> Who bow to a crowned thing,
> To a puppet they call a King.
> To arms! Republicans!
> Strike now for Liberty!
> March on: march on: Republicans!
> We march to victory.[53]

The republican movement, however, had already suffered a blow from which it did not recover. The Prince of Wales nearly died, on December 14, 1871, from typhoid. That day was the tenth anniversary of the Prince Consort's death, and there was a great burst of sympathy for the Queen, who had rushed to Sandringham to be at her son's bedside. The sudden collapse of republicanism showed the tremendous reserve strength of the monarchy. The basic conservatism of a prosperous, religious, form-conscious people felt at home with the monarchy, and with the dutiful, prudent, family-oriented Queen. Although the *Times*'s comments may seem slightly sentimental today, they were probably just what the public craved. Column after column described the concern of the nation, and there was a desire expressed "not [to] profane [the Queen's grief] by coarse intrusion," especially on a day of such painful memory and of such horrible new possiblities:

> For ten long years has today been a day of saddest meditation with the *Queen*, the day of remembrance of the dead. Her sons and daugh-

ters have assembled about her at Windsor, and mother and children have knelt together in the precious sepulchre love has built to receive the remains of their lost husband and father, there to pour out their hearts at the shrine of undying affection.[54]

When Sir Charles Dilke moved in the Commons in March 1872 for a full inquiry into the Queen's finances, he was ignominiously defeated; amid tumultuous applause Gladstone delivered an affirmation of his faith in the monarchy. And Lord Henry Lennox, a leading member of the Conservative party, wrote to Disraeli, "What a sell for Dilke this illness has been."[55] It is worth noting that within a few months Disraeli delivered his Crystal Palace speech, with its explicit imperialism; the Queen, by her death three decades later, was to be associated in the closest possible manner with the Empire. Moreover, Charles Dilke, who had been ostracized by London society for his republicanism, went on to become a close friend of the Prince of Wales; and Joseph Chamberlain, who left the Liberal party in the mid-1880s over the issue of Irish Home Rule, (and was followed by men like Peter Alfred Taylor and George Dixon), went on to become the high priest of British imperialism. Republicanism had no place to go; it was, depending upon one's point of view, either repulsive or irrelevant.

It cannot, however, be disregarded. It demonstrates that even midway in her reign Victoria was not the sanctified figure she was at her death. It also demonstrates that she never understood one of the vital aspects of modern monarchy. Royalty must be interesting, and the Queen, with her complete removal from even the slightest contact with everyday life, never realized this. Nothing shows her imperviousness to public opinion better than the affair of John Brown. From the mid-1860s until his death in 1883 John Brown, a Scottish servant of the Queen, had a mysterious hold over her. Any criticism of him only strengthened the Queen in her conviction that the upper classes did not understand or practice or even recognize virtue. From 1865 to 1870 the scandal over Brown was at its height; it was rumored that Victoria was his mistress or his wife, and she was commonly referred to as "Mrs. Brown" or the "Empress Brown." He was an exceptionally crude man, despised by much of the royal family, and a favorite subject of the satirical press. But the more Brown was criticized the more stubborn the Queen became in her defense of him, and the more determined she was to maintain her seclusion and her prolonged mourning for Albert; thus the problem of John Brown is closely connected with that of the republican movement. At his death the Court Circular devoted twenty-five lines to a eulogy of Brown; this compared with the five lines which had been devoted to Disraeli in 1881.[56]

It follows from this that court life under Victoria was an incredible round of tedium. Sir Henry Campbell-Bannerman wrote to his wife of a visit to Balmoral:

It is the funniest life conceivable: like a convent. We meet at meals, breakfast at 9:45, lunch, dinner 9: and when we are finished, each is off to his cell (at least I to mine) and there is no common life except

round a table. About 7 a man comes round and says whether I am
to dine with the Queen.[57]

The Queen's prejudices and whims ruled Osborne, Windsor, and Balmoral, and she actually seemed to take pride in her removal from the eyes
of her subjects. None of this means, of course, that the Queen was indifferent to the ceremonies of her court; they had to be carried out with the
greatest possible precision and flair. The Queen herself, moreover, was a
most imposing figure—short and dumpy though she may have been—who
unquestionably added to the awesomeness of any royal occasion.[58] The
Prince of Wales was clearly in awe of his mother, who would tolerate no
untoward behavior of any kind on his part. But above all, things rarely
changed at her Court. Commands to "dine and sleep" filled the hardiest
statesman with trepidation. Conversation was subdued, and when the
Queen put down her knife and fork the plates of all the guests were
removed whether they had finished or not.[59] Smoking, like divorce, was
regarded as a particularly horrible sin. Notices were hung on the walls at
Windsor instructing gentlemen not to smoke, and those who did so anyway were wise to suck lozenges before entering the royal presence. Once a
man was seen lying in his pajamas on his bedroom floor blowing smoke
from his cigar up the chimney. In fact, the oddities of the Victorian court
make fascinating reading,[60] for one gets a picture of a world with virtually
no connection with outside life, except in the realm of high politics. The
Queen was clearly a shrewd, and at times most realistic woman, with unex-
pected streaks of kindness and understanding along with her quite as-
tounding selfishness. But one is struck by the difficulty that the monarchy
would have had in the twentieth century had not another reign transformed English court life.

Yet Victoria did become the quintessence of her country. In the public
mind throne and nation became one, and it happened in spite of her,
because she never catered to anyone. Of course this may have been part of
her secret: She was so obviously above corrupt influence or vulgar desire
that it was difficult to think of her otherwise than as a great institution.
The last decades of her reign, furthermore, coincided with imperial
greatness, which stimulated the patriotism which is so much to the advantage of the Crown. The monarchy also, of course, helped to create an
awareness of imperial grandeur, by providing a focus for loyalty in the context of Empire. In other words, the monarchy was in the right place at the
right time, and was able to take advantage of the opportunities thus offered.

The opportunities were not political, as there was no way for the
monarchy to continue to play a central role in political life. The growth of
the electorate and the development of the party system greatly reduced
the opportunities of the throne for maneuver, although, to this day, some
room for doing so remains. Victoria did understand the vital importance
of demanding that her ministers communicate with her at all times, and so
she was able, as were her successors, to use accumulated knowledge to

good effect. But to try to decide the extent of royal influence over political affairs, and to compare the degree of that influence in 1837 with 1861 or with 1901 is beside the point.[61]

What is important is the new dimension of the monarchy's importance. Today, because of Victoria's legacy, the monarchy acts to legitimize change; it conceals, or at least makes easier for the nation as a whole to accept, measures of a fundamental nature. This is perhaps why a recent observer has called the monarchy "an integral part of a flexible and progressive society."[62] It is true that the monarchy, and the make-up of the Court, can have a deadening effect on society by diverting many people from a realization of the necessity of change;[63] it may also have, as an American ambassador noted a few years after Victoria's death, great importance "in keeping the vested interest of the aristocratic social structure secure,"[64] by enforcing on the nation an essentially conservative frame of reference. But it is just as true that by cushioning change the monarchy has eased many of the strains of the nineteenth and twentieth centuries.

The psychological role of the monarchy is also great in that it denies the highest position in the state to politicians. This performs the important role of dividing the emotional, sentimental, and patriotic aspect of national life from the political. When these aspects come together the result can be highly dangerous, for when a political leader can control both of them the opportunities open to him expand greatly. Under Victoria the role of the sovereign became "less to exercise power than to keep power in its proper proportion to the totality of life."[65] The sovereign, although much less powerful than the Prime Minister, is, in one sense, far more important, for he represents the nation in all its aspects, and not just politically. To a considerable extent this is a legacy of Victoria, for, without fully understanding what she was doing, she transformed the monarchy from an essentially political to an essentially social and psychological institution.

In his comments on the monarchy Walter Bagehot wrote that one of the most important features of the dignified capacity of the Queen was to make government intelligible.[66] Although Bagehot wrote over a century ago, his comments are by no means dated, for they point toward one of the most crucial roles of the modern monarchy. Victoria found herself in a position to combat much of the alienation, or *anomie*, of modern life. The sovereign made government, and the nation, and much of one's entire experience, understandable. A human point of reference appeared, which was far more satisfactory than any abstraction could ever be. In order to make life intelligible men crave to identify with someone, and in England that someone has become, much to the advantage of the state, a figure who is neutral in politics. As Sebastian de Grazia has observed, "The *ruler's* power of reassurance over the political community is one of immeasurable importance. Ordinarily it can scarcely be discerned in people. Yet let an extraordinary event occur, though but the mere presence of supreme authority, and emotions stand out more clearly, like a flat map put in relief." De Grazia quotes a long passage from Virginia Woolf's *Mrs. Dalloway* in which the kind of reaction he is discussing takes place.[67] The focusing of these passions and needs on the throne has been one of the greatest sources of its strength; this phenomenon was at the core of the late Victorian monarchy, and has been passed down to the present.

Victoria was thus the founder of the institution of monarchy as we know it today. Admittedly it was an accidental founding, and the opportunities she and her successors were able to take advantage of were not of their own making. But she left behind an institution far more subtle than most of her contemporaries realized. Harold Laski was quite right when he wrote that "the metaphysics of limited monarchy do not easily lend themselves to critical discussion;"[68] he was also correct when he called the Crown "a pervasive agent . . . which no student of the Constitution can afford to ignore."[69] The metaphysics and the pervasiveness are really what make the monarchy so fascinating, and even mysterious, and they were clearly in evidence in the latter part of the nineteenth century. But they were not enough, and something else was needed before the necessary ingredients for survival were at hand. Fortunately that something else was to be supplied by Albert Edward, Prince of Wales.

---

[1] On George IV see Roger Fulford's biography, *George IV*. On William IV see Fulford's *Hanover to Windsor*, chapter 1, and W. Gore Allen, *William IV*. One should also consult Fulford's *The Royal Dukes*. On Victoria's youth, as on all other periods of her life, see Elizabeth Longford, *Victoria R.I.*

[2] Norman Gash, *Reaction and Reconstruction in English Politics, 1832–1852*, p. 5. The following discussion is indebted to Gash's analysis.

[3] *Ibid.*, pp. 27–28.

[4] *Ibid.*, p. 29. See also Frank Eyck, *The Prince Consort*, p. 253.

[5] *The Letters of Queen Victoria*, second series, I, xiii.

[6] *The Quarterly Review*, CXCIII (1901), p. 337. The article was actually written by Sir Edmund Gosse.

[7] G. M. Young, *Victorian England, Portrait of an Age* (London, 1960), p. 141.

[8] Robert Blake, *Disraeli and Gladstone*, pp. 33–34.

[9] Lytton Strachey, *Queen Victoria* (London, 1948), pp. 179–80.

[10] See Maurice V. Brett, editor, *Journals and Letters of Reginald Viscount Esher*, II, 99. Among Albert's lesser-known accomplishments are his songs, which one critic has called "far better than any of the Mendelssohn Lied." Moreover, it is argued that his piano accompaniments rival the best of Schubert's. See Heuwell Tircuit, in "This World," p. 34, *San Francisco Chronicle*, April 12, 1970. Of course, Albert's interest in the arts embraced far more than music.

[11] *Letters of Queen Victoria*, third series, II, 384.

[12] *Ibid.*, second series, II, 315.

[13] *Ibid.*, second series, II, 166.

[14] *Ibid.*, third series, II, 168.

[15] Philip Guedalla, editor, *The Queen and Mr. Gladstone*, I, 227.

[16] Quoted in Frank Hardie, *The Political Influence of Queen Victoria*, p. 140.

[17] Quoted in Viscount Chilston, *W. H. Smith* , p. 94.

[18] Quoted in Kenneth Rose, *Superior Person*, p. 327.

[19] Frank Hardie, *The Political Influence of the British Monarchy*, p. 56.

[20] On this entire matter see Frank Hardie, *The Political Influence of Queen Victoria*, especially pp. 124ff.

[21] See Frank Hardie, *The Political Influence of the British Monarchy*, p. 57.

[22] *Ibid.*, pp. 20–21, and Frank Hardie, *The Political Influence of Queen Victoria*, pp. 178ff.

[23] Lady Gwendolen Cecil, *Life of Robert Marquis of Salisbury*, III, 185.

[24] *Letters of Queen Victoria*, third series, I, 140–41.

[25] Andre Maurois, *The Edwardian Era*, pp. 4–5.

[26] Zara Steiner, *The Foreign Office and Foreign Affairs, 1898–1914*, p. 200.

[27] *Ibid.*

[28] *Ibid.*, p. 201, quoting from J. A. S. Grenville, *Lord Salisbury and Foreign Policy*, p. 333.

[29] Lady Gwendolen Cecil, *Life of Robert Marquis of Salisbury*, III, 182.

30 *Letters of Queen Victoria*, third series, III, 392.
31 Lady Gwendolen Cecil, *Life of Robert Marquis of Salisbury*.
32 Philip Guedalla, editor, *The Queen and Mr. Gladstone*, I, 201. The Queen was upset at the idea of treating Roman Catholic peers "on an equality with the Protestants."
33 The best discussion of the Queen and the Church is Owen Chadwick, *The Victorian Church*, I, 158–66, II, 328–42. See also Frank Hardie, *The Political Influence of Queen Victoria*, pp. 132–37, and Dudley W. R. Bahlman, "The Queen, Mr. Gladstone, and Church Patronage," *Victorian Studies*, III (1960), 349–380. Bahlman argues that one of the many reasons for the antipathy between the Queen and Gladstone was their conflict over ecclesiastical appointments, about which both felt passionately.
34 Owen Chadwick, *The Victorian Church*, II, 330–31.
35 W. E. Monypenny and G. E. Buckle, *The Life of Benjamin Disraeli*, two-volume edition (London, 1929), II, 398.
36 *Ibid.*, II, 334–35, 340. See also Robert Blake, *Disraeli*, p. 511.
37 John W. Wheeler-Bennett, *King George VI*, p. 10.
38 Gilbert Chesterton, "The Queen," *The Westminister Review*, CLV (1901), pp. 237, 239.
39 Naomi Bliven, "Babes in the Wood," *The New Yorker*, March 23, 1968, p. 157. This comment was written about Victoria's granddaughter, Alix of Hesse, the last Czarina of Russia, and her husband, Nicholas II, but it applies just as much to Victoria herself.
40 Philip Magnus, *Gladstone*, pp. 208ff.
41 Quoted in W.E. Monypenny and G. E. Buckle, *The Life of Benjamin Disraeli*, two-volume edition (London, 1929), II, 483.
   It was in this speech that Disraeli made a slip, which caused him much embarrassment, when he said that the Queen was "physically and morally incapacitated from performing her duties." He needed all his tact to soothe the Queen.
42 J. L. Garvin, *The Life of Joseph Chamberlain*, I, 152.
43 *Ibid.*
44 Quoted in Stephen Gwynn and Gertrude Tuckwell, *The Life of the Rt. Hon. Sir Charles Dilke*, I, 140.
45 See Frank Hardie, *The Political Influence of Queen Victoria*, p. 208.
46 November 9, 1871.
47 *Parliamentary Debates*, third series, CCVIII, 579.
48 *Ibid.*, 584.
49 See Frank Hardie, *The Political Influence of Queen Victoria*, pp. 208–09.
50 Quoted in Hypatia Bradlaugh Bonner, *Charles Bradlaugh*, I, 310.
51 On Bradlaugh and the republican movement see Walter Arnstein, *The Bradlaugh Case*, pp. 19–20; and Sir Sidney Lee, *King Edward VII*, I, 328–29.
52 Frederick Harrison, "The Monarchy," *The Fortnightly Review*, XI, new series (1872), pp. 634–41.
53 Quoted in Crane Brinton, *English Political Thought in the Nineteenth Century*, p. 243.
54 December 14, 1871.
55 See Sir Sidney Lee, *King Edward VII*, I, 329.
56 On John Brown see Elizabeth Longford, *Victoria R.I.*, chapter XXIII; and Tom Cullen, *The Empress Brown*.
57 Quoted in J. A. Spender, *The Life of Sir Henry Campbell-Bannerman*, I, 168.
58 Interested readers can find splendid collections of royal pictures in the following books: Helmut and Alison Gernsheim, *Victoria R* (New York, 1959); also their *Edward VII and Queen Alexandra* (London, 1962); and H. Tatlock Miller and Loudon Sainthill, *Undoubted Queen* (New York, 1958).
59 E. S. Turner, *The Court of St. James's*, p. 333.
60 Among the many accounts are *ibid.*, chapters 26–29; Christopher Hibbert, *The Court at Windsor*, Part 5; Sir Frederick Ponsonby, *Recollections of Three Reigns* (New York 1952), Book I; Mary Lutyens, editor, *Lady Lytton's Court Diary, 1895–1899*; and Victor Mallet, editor, *Life With Queen Victoria, Marie Mallet's Letters from Court, 1887–1901*.
61 See Frank Hardie, *The Political Influence of Queen Victoria*, p. 237, where he argues that while the *power* of the monarchy declined during Victoria's reign its *influence* increased. He attacks Lytton Strachey for stating that the Crown was weaker at the Queen's death than at any other time; Hardie claims that it was weakest at Victoria's accession, not death.
62 Drew Middleton, *These Are the British*, p. 33.
63 On this subject see Kingsley Martin, *The Crown and the Establishment*.
64 Quoted in Burton J. Hendrick, *The Life and Letters of Walter H. Page*, III, 111.
65 Dermot Morrah, *The Work of the Queen*, p. 38.
66 *The English Constitution*, p. 10.
67 Sebastian de Grazia, *The Political Community, a Study of Anomie*, pp. 110–12.
68 *Parliamentary Government in England*, p. 388.
69 *The Crisis and the Constitution*, p. 31.

CHAPTER 2

THE EDWARDIAN MONARCHY

Albert Edward, as Prince of Wales and as King, did not fit the Victorian conception of monarchy. He personified no traditional virtues; he exuded no middle-class morality. To a great extent, in fact, he represented the antithesis of everything his mother had stood for. Yet he brought to the monarchy a strength and an appeal which contributed greatly to its popularity in the twentieth century, and which, paradoxically, was completely compatible with the legacy of his parents.

None of this, however, was planned. Victoria and Albert decided, as soon as he was born, to make the heir to the throne a model of everything that the best nineteenth-century educational techniques could achieve. He was going to be studious, moral, and dutiful. To achieve all this the Prince Consort "devised for his eldest son an educational plan of unparalleled rigour which made no allowance for human weakness."[1] But, while "the Princess Royal was an extremely intelligent child, . . . Bertie, though he was good humoured and gentle, seemed to display a deep-seated repugnance to every sort of mental exertion."[2] The Queen and her husband were deeply distressed by this, and rejected the sensible advice of Lord Melbourne, who cautioned Victoria not to be "oversolicitious about education. It may mould and direct the character, but it rarely alters it."[3] So they pushed on, and it is certainly probable that their efforts to make the young prince "a model of morality, of piety, of deportment, and of intellectual accomplishment" were "not wholly beneficial to his development."[4]

It seems clear that the results of the educational pressures to which the future Edward VII was subjected were the opposite of what had been intended. The future King schemed for indolence. This is understandable, for Prince Albert drafted elaborate regulations for him and for his tutors, and wrote long exhortations to his son about the most minute matters of conduct. Practically no contact with children of his own age was allowed, and his studies were very dull indeed. Even the novels of Sir Walter Scott were banned as demoralizing, and the study of history, so important to a child destined to ascend the British throne, was reduced to a long and tedious catalogue of dates. Probably nothing could have made Edward VII into a royal John Stuart Mill, but if the pressures had been a little less he might not have sought pleasure and avoided work with such determination for the remainder of his life.

Yet, in spite of his "singular incapacity to apply his mind to any sort of study for half an hour," the future King was able to remember what he learned through conversation.[5] His early visits to Paris and to the United States, moreover, were well-received, but these early displays of charm did not impress his mother, who distrusted him, and perhaps, deep in her heart, even disliked him. It is probable that Victoria blamed her eldest son for Albert's death, as it was hastened by the exertions of a trip to Cambridge to straighten out the ill-effects of one of the Prince's early scandals. Certainly the gloom of his mother's court horrified the young Prince and hastened his plunge into a world of fashionable frivolity. Victoria was genuinely scandalized by her son's life; she disliked and distrusted "society," and thought much of the aristocracy hopelessly irresponsible. She longed for her son to surround himself with "really good, steady, and distinguished people,"[6] the sort of people Albert admired. The Queen feared that the worst features of her uncles were coming out in her son.

Much of the blame, however, for the Prince's frivolous and social life rests with Victoria herself. The Queen absolutely refused to give her son any significant work to do; it was not until the last fifteen years of her reign that he was allowed to see state papers regularly; a century later, another Prince of Wales was reading state papers while still in his early twenties. Gladstone urged the Queen, much to her displeasure, to give the Prince something to do; in fact, the matter of the Prince's unemployment took up a disproportionate amount of the Prime Minister's time. But one must also sympathize with Victoria; there is evidence that the Prince's tendency toward gossip might well have endangered state secrets. Lord Granville, the Foreign Secretary, wrote to Henry Ponsonby in 1871 that the Prince "asked me to keep him informed during the war. One evening I got four messages from different friends telling me to be careful. One of my first notes to him had been handed round a dinner party."[7] Furthermore, in spite of his frequent requests to be given something to do, his habits made it difficult even to approach him on matters of importance. The Queen's secretary thought that while the Prince was "genial and pleasant . . . for a few minutes," he did "not endure. He cannot keep up interest for any length of time and I don't think he will ever settle down to business." Moreover, "to get the Prince of Wales to enter into a subject or decide on it is most difficult. [Secretaries] have to catch snap answers from him as he goes out shooting, etc. Then he runs off . . . to Trouville where of course business is impossible."[8] One of the Prince's few significant acts of governmental service did not take place until 1884, when he sat on the Royal Commission on the Housing of the Working Classes. He attended 19 of its 51 meetings, and was deeply moved by much of what h :

saw and heard. He might have had a better attendance record but for the death of his brother, Prince Leopold, and the wedding of his niece, Victoria of Hesse. However, he did not travel to Homburg that autumn in order to go to the Commission's meetings.[9]

Nevertheless, it was during his early years of unemployment that the Prince established the reputation for charm and gaiety that has made his name ever since a synonym for all the pleasures of a world that has disappeared in the twentieth century. It was his overpowering charm that captivated most of those with whom he came into contact. As Arthur Ponsonby has written:

> It would be quite impossible to overestimate what amounted to genius. It is not too much to say that in spite of drawbacks, faults and failures, it *made* him. With a dignified presence, a fine profile . . . and a courtly manner, he never missed saying a word to the humblest visitor, attentant or obscure official. He would enter a room and, with the skill of an accomplished billiard player, look forward several strokes, so that no one was left out. The appropriate remark, the telling serious phrase and amusing joke, accompanied by a gurgling laugh to a close friend, made all delighted even to watch him.[10]

It may have been, of course, that this charm was purely superficial, a façade with practically nothing behind, as Ponsonby argues, but it was none the less a façade that created a devastating impression, and gave even the most experienced men the conviction that the Prince was as knowledgeable and sophisticated as they.

The Princess of Wales was also a great practitioner of charm. The future Queen Alexandra was raised very simply and in relative poverty in Copenhagen. Her father, who was to become Christian IX of Denmark, was anything but a glamorous or important figure, and he never suspected that one of his daughters would become the Queen of England, another the Czarina of Russia, and a younger son the King of Greece. It took considerable time before Victoria, ably assisted by her daughter, the Crown Princess of Prussia, settled on Alexandra as a wife for young Albert Edward, expecially as a Danish marriage might be taken as a insult to Prussia; Prussian-Danish relations soon culminated in war. But her availability and simplicty triumphed, and in 1863, at Windsor, in the presence of a weeping Victoria, Alexandra became the Princess of Wales.

There is no doubt that she played a central, if entirely unconscious, role in the evolution of the British monarchy. She added greatly to her husband's aura of charm. She provided him, as seemed entirely appropriate, with a wife of great beauty and presence. She could go nowhere without being the center of attention; with no effort at all she set styles and instituted fads. If she wore a diamond choker to conceal a scar on her neck, diamond chokers became the rage. If she limped because of an illness, the "Alexandra limp" was copied everywhere in smart society. Her love of fun, which largely derived from her childhood in Copenhagen, and her complete lack of interest in anything serious, made her a perfect mistress for Marlborough House. Her only strong political view was a passionate hatred of Prussia, and particularly the House of Hohenzollern, for depriving her father of Schleswig-Holstein. Her understanding and tolerance of her husband's extra-marital affairs, climaxed when she led Mrs. Keppel to Edward VII's deathbed, made her the ideal symbol of a more permissive age. Certainly her beauty made her a splendid centerpiece for the magnificence of Edwardian court life.

But this is only part of the story. Alexandra was, above all, interested in her children. As a mother she was anything but frivolous. She gave her children an intense love that marked their entire lives, and her influence was central in the formation of the character of her second son, the future George V. His domesticity, his simple virtues, and his devotion to work, the importance of which will be emphasized below, came in large part from his "motherdear," whose love he returned without qualification. Alexandra was, accordingly, only partly "Edwardian"; the close ties that characterized her childhood always remained part of her, and she, as much as anyone else, gave the British royal family that air of mutual devotion which, even when expressed in rather awesome terms, has been of such importance in this century. In fact, as Alexandra became older, and her deafness, which had started to afflict her early in life, became worse, she turned more and more toward her children and intimate friends for companionship. It is probable, moreover, that Alexandra, although by no means an intellectual woman, was anything but the rather insipid character she is often portrayed as; her deafness made her conversation so vague that an erroneous impression of stupidity emerged.[11]

Attractive as charm and gaiety may be, most Victorians probably shared their Queen's view that they were not sufficient qualifications for a future King. And this unfavorable impression of the Prince of Wales was greatly strengthened by a series of scandals in which the Prince found himself. These scandals left an "undercurrent of resentment" against him, to use Sir Sidney Lee's phrase, which never disappeared. The first of these scandals was the Mordaunt divorce case. Lady Mordaunt was a close friend of the Prince, who called on her often at her house, where they were frequently quite alone. Unfortunately Lady Mordaunt was slowly going insane. When she gave birth to a child she somehow received the impression that it was blind; crazed with horror, she "confessed" to her husband that the child was not his. Although not believing her at first, he eventually became suspicious, and upon discovering some of the Prince's letters to his wife, sued for divorce, naming as co-respondents two close friends of the Prince's; Albert Edward himself was called as a witness, the allegation being that the co-respondents had confessed their misdeeds to him. The case received tremendous publicity, especially after some of the Prince's letters to Lady Mordaunt were produced in court; they proved to be harmless, but the horror of divorce was so great in 1870 that the Prince was nonetheless seriously compromised. He was asked point-blank in court if there had ever been any "improper familiarity or criminal act" between him and Lady Mordaunt, and his emphatic denial was received with applause, but the damage was done; the heir to the throne had appeared in a suit for divorce.

The next great blow to the Prince's reputation also involved matrimonial irregularity. In the autumn of 1875 Albert Edward was sent off to India, and he took along one of his close friends, the Earl of Aylesford. Whether the Earl was taken along for companionship, or because it was feared that, were he left behind, he would learn of the attentions that had been paid to his wife by the Prince, is not known for certain; it is known, however, that shortly after the departure the somewhat dissolute Marquess of Blandford became "devoted" to Lady Aylesford. Her husband, upon learning of this development, returned to England; when the Prince of Wales arrived home he severely criticized Blandford's conduct. At this point the Marquess's brother, Lord Randolph Churchill, intervened; and he intimated to the Prince that, unless his criticism stopped, his letters to Lady Aylesford would be made public. In response Albert Edward challenged Lord Randolph to a duel; discretion prevailed and this potentially most interesting event never occurred, but the Prince declared that he would never set foot in any house that received the Churchills. This was of course a grave matter for the Churchill family; to understate the case, it could result in a considerable diminution of their social life; this, in turn, would certainly have serious consequences for Lord Randolph's political future, simply because so much practical politics was conducted in a social setting. The result of this unattractive affair was the despatch of the Duke of Marlborough, Blandford and Lord Randolph's father, to Dublin as Viceroy; Lord Randolph, his American wife, and their young son Winston all followed the Duke into exile. It was several years before the breach was healed.

The third scandal, and the most celebrated one, was the baccarat affair. The Prince of Wales, who was fond of gambling, had gone off to play baccarat at Tranby-Croft, the house of his good friend Sir Arthur Wilson. One evening Sir Arthur's son thought he saw Sir William Gordon Cumming, a colonel of the Scots Guards, cheating. He conveyed this suspicion to another guest, a subaltern in Sir William's regiment. They proceeded to keep a close watch on Sir William, and when they both saw him cheating, Sir Arthur's son told his mother, sister, and brother-in-law. The following night all five watched Sir William closely and caught him cheating yet again. At this point two other guests, Lady Coventry and General Owen Williams, were told, and it was decided to inform the Prince, rather than handle the matter themselves. The outcome was that Sir William signed a pledge promising never to play cards for money again; in return, no one else was to be told of the cheating. Whether Sir William, in signing the pledge, acknowledged guilt, or was simply acting to avoid scandal, has never been settled.

The secret leaked out, possibly through indiscretion, possibly because of a rumor that Sir William had broken his end of the bargain, making the others feel that they were accordingly released from their pledge of secrecy. An extremely embarrassing situation arose, because under army regulations there should have been a military enquiry. Sir William then brought an action for slander against the five who had told Lady Coventry and the General, and in June 1891 the Prince again found himself in court as a witness. Just as he was leaving the box, after an uneventful examination, he was asked by a juror if he believed the charges against Sir William to be true; the Prince replied that he had no alternative but to believe them, as they were so strongly supported. After that, the verdict was never in doubt.

This episode was by no means treated lightly at the time. It was held to be dangerous to the very survival of the monarchy, especially as the Prince, with the Queen approaching eighty, could succeed to the throne at any time. Radical papers, which had opposed an increase in the Prince's allowance two years before, now claimed that the people were paying his gambling debts. The *Times* was horrified that baccarat had been played to please the Prince; the fact that his set was a gambling set, and that the "most visible embodiment of the Monarchial principle" next to the Queen herself had acted so badly, could be very dangerous, especially "in these democratic days." The *Daily News* wanted the Prince bound to "a pure, a simple, and a cleanly life"; the *Liverpool Courier* thought it "unedifying" to have the future King officiating at "a gambler's orgy—shuffling the cards for five pound notes"; The *Nottingham Express* even thought that the British Empire had been humiliated. But Victoria, who was still the supreme symbol of the monarchy, looked all the better in comparison.[12]

These scandals, furthermore, were taking place in the midst of what seemed to many people a world of complete irresponsibility. The Prince and Princess of Wales were, many of their future subjects thought, utterly undignified. But it must be remembered that, for all its social change, the late Victorian and Edwardian world was very tempting and pleasant for the rich and well-born, and Albert Edward made little effort to ward off temptation. He was surrounded, in fact, by a group of people who made a career of presenting him with temptation.

In his world, for example, practical jokes were the vogue. Lillie Langtry, one of the Prince's mistresses, boasted of how she told her host that the soup was cold; he then angrily took a swallow and badly burned his mouth. The Duchess of Marlborough wrote that her mother-in-law once gave a dinner party when she put small bits of soap among the real pieces of cheese; this same merry woman once tied an inkpot over a door—the inkpot emptying its contents on her husband's head. Apple-pie beds and leaking hot-water bottles were ordinary features of life in the Marlborough House set. Once Lady de Grey bought a whole set of china so a footman could drop it and make Lord de Grey think that he had lost his priceless collection. Lillie Langtry dressed up as a hawker and sold matches in the street; the Princess of Pless was so used to "larks" that she once mistook an earthquake for a jokester under her bed. At times, of course, the jokes seem to have been done without humor or gaiety, but rather with crudity and cruelty. Unsympathetic observers can paint a revolting picture of the Prince, pouring brandy down a friend's neck like a spoiled child whom no one dared criticize. Demanding to be entertained, ruining his friends' bank accounts with his whims, Edward VII did not always have even an attractive façade. He was often arrogant, and much as he enjoyed frivolity he would not tolerate even the most trivial liberty with his position. As George Dangerfield put it, "It was unwise to assume that the King's behavior took after his morality. Only the latter was loose." Any *faux pas*, moreover, could bring social disaster; a woman who tripped over her train at a court ball was off the court list forever. Equal disaster could come if one bored the Prince, and he was easily bored; when he started to drum irritable fingers on the arm of his chair someone's social position was in grave danger. Yet he could show great tact and kindness; once he threw asparagus over his shoulder at a state dinner in order not to embarrass an Indian Prince who had done so first.[13]

Many Englishmen were also disturbed at the Prince's sexual life. It was increasingly realized that he did not live up to the standards set by his mother. Even if nothing specific was known by the great majority of his future subjects, the fact that this aspect of his life more closely resembled that of his Hanoverian great-uncles than that of his parents was clearly sensed. His relations with women like Lady Brooke and, later, Mrs. Keppel, represented a major break with the standards which Albert would have liked to see in his eldest son; in fact, the early scandal that contributed to the Prince Consort's death involved an unfortunate indiscretion of Albert Edward's with an actress. This is not to say that Victorian England was a country of outstanding purity; recent research into the Victorian "underworld" has shown that quite the contrary was true; nevertheless, the kind of upper-class life depicted in Victoria Sackville-West's *The Edwardians*, with hostesses understandingly placing lovers near their mistresses during long and gluttonous countryhouse weekends, represented a substantial break with mid-Victorian conventions. Of course, everyone was expected to observe certain outward formalities; the Prince of Wales himself was particularly conscious of this necessity; for the old Queen, however, and those like her, mere outward formalities were quite inadequate.

It is therefore no surprise that Albert Edward's accession was greeted, to say the least, with modified rapture. His charm was well known and widely acknowledged; his personal life and character raised doubts. Henry James probably spoke for many when he said that "we are to have no more of little mysterious Victoria, but instead fat vulgar dreadful Edward." Although the press poured conventional compliments on the new King, it also, sometimes subtly, sometimes crudely, sent pious warning in his direction. *The Spectator*, for example, warned that he must never forget that his life was now consecrated to the national service; what might be pardoned in a Prince cannot be condoned in a sovereign. The *Times* showed itself willing to forgive but not immediately to forget past indiscretions when it admitted that a person in the difficult position of Heir Apparent must "offer up the familiar prayer, 'Lead us not into Temptation,'" with "a feeling akin to hopelessness."

Many English feared that monstrosities of behavior would be perpetrated by the new King, who rather pointedly decided to call himself Edward VII, instead of Albert I. The future was certainly clouded:

> The dear, brave old lady has gone, and those of us who ever stop to *think* know that England can never be *quite the same* again.
>
> I am thunderstruck to hear the new King—heartless fellow!—has been proclaimed Edward the Seventh. It is *quite quite* wrong! He promised his dear mama in accordance with his papa's wishes, that he would come to the throne as *Albert Edward.* Now he is to be Edward the Seventh! It's quite shocking. How mortifying it is of the wicked man, and what a *shocking* start to a new reign, but *thank God, his poor mama knows nothing of it!*
>
> ... I hope your blinds are properly drawn. ... This is no time for modern disgression.[14]

This view from the squirearchy of Warwickshire was echoed throughout the nation. Much of the middle class, and a large segment of the older aristocracy, deplored what they feared would be the triumph of that supreme ideal of the Marlborough House set, smartness. They wondered if established society could maintain itself, in what was clearly going to be a difficult and dangerous new century, under the sway of what Rudyard Kipling called "a corpulent voluptuary." Ancient lineage or a great name might well mean nothing at court or in society from now on, especially as the King was known to enjoy the company of people like American plutocrats, international bankers, Jewish tradesmen, and veldt millionaires. Were old families, who had contributed for centuries to the building of the nation, going to have to bankrupt themselves in order to keep up with the new rich? Indeed, from the 1870s on that tendency had been well enough in evidence. More and more those Englishmen who stood by old values would live in isolation, maintaining a way and style of life "with the same unruffled tenacity with which the Sephardic community at Salonika persisted in speaking fifteenth-century Spanish."[15] As for the middle classes, many of them saw the smartness of their new King as the ultimate in vulgarity, and as the complete negation of those principles of duty, work, thrift, and honor which were responsible for England's greatness, and which Queen Victoria, with her perfect sense of value, had so well understood and had so flawlessly embodied in her own life.

Yet Edward VII turned out to be one of the most successful and popular Kings of modern times. He gave the monarchy a new basis for survival in the twentieth century; eventually his legacy, in the person of his son, accommodated itself to Victorian principles, and the essence of the modern monarchy came into being. In an extraordinary way Edward VII fulfilled a modern need, and gave the monarchy a dimension that allowed it to be what Walter Bagehot, a third of a century before, had seen was so necessary. That dimension was simply interest: Edward and Alexandra were fascinating and glamorous; they were accordingly able to fill a gap in modern life, and to personalize government and the nation. Edward VII, in fact, made the monarchy real in the sense of making it a part of everyday life. There was something of the universal uncle in him, a benevolent, faintly disreputable, easily understood uncle.[16] Moreover, his "human weaknesses, which good taste banned from the written word, helped to make the round, human character, even to heighten the impression of kingliness."[17] Much of the triumph of the Edwardian monarchy, therefore, was not based on the brilliance and insight of a shrewd sovereign, but rather on an accidental public relations triumph, in which the innate vulgarity of a spoiled old man perfectly complemented the innate vulgarity of a curious world.

One of the first acts of the new King was to move into Buckingham Palace, a place Victoria had disliked and had for several decades rarely used. With little restraint the rooms of the Palace were cleaned out, Court personnel changed, and everything made ready for the ostentation which so well suited the new King.[18] Indeed, "the effect upon the remnants of the Victorians was . . . much as if a Viennese hussar had suddenly burst into an English vicarage."[19] It may be that a novelist can best capture the feeling:

> And now came Edward in his Daimler. The picture is symbolical, for the motoring age would not begin for another twenty years. Yet the symbol was prophetic and fateful. There the King sat, goggled, dustcoated, high up in that entracing seat. He clutched the wheel, and the ladies beside him in their wide hats and their thick white veils which made them look like instruments for diabolo. There they sat, propelled possibly by steam or by other ingenious and preposterous features; they sat, foreshadowing the future.

It certainly seems that

> . . . in the days between January 22nd and February 1st in 1901, something was passing out of England. An essence, feeling or attitude; something like a ghost, visible, but not tangible; something indeed which seemed easy of apprehension to all the senses except the humblest one, the sense of touch; it was going out of England like a mammoth, like the Romans, like hydrogen from a bottle.[20]

There can be little doubt that coming to the throne was a great tonic to Edward VII which allowed him to let his personality, so long in the shadow of his mother, expand on a broad stage. He had "the vital elixir of zest. To whatever he applied himself he gave his whole heart; he did it with every nerve and fiber."[21] By 1901 it seemed as if the English were, perhaps more than they realized it themselves, ready to cast off "the perfect model of English motherhood," and to accept a man who "had become, they believed, the most genial type of sporting English gentleman."[22]

Edward VII, in fact, managed to profit both from the desire for the preservation of the status quo and from the desire for change. He was old, his life stretched back over many decades and thus suggested continuity and tradition; yet the new spirit which had crept into English life "was . . . openly manifest in the new King. It was an amused, an expansive spirit." Furthermore, amid the uncertainty of the Boer War, he appeared as "a supremely self-confident man . . . he looked like a sporting banker, a living testament to the fact that the nation's credit was still sound."[23]

This self-confidence was central to his success. It was a reaffirmation of the glory of Victorian England, at just the time when such a reaffirmation was desperately needed. Clearly the age of "splendid isolation" was coming to an end; diplomatically, economically, and soon even on the seas, England was no longer unchallenged. At home the political climate was increasingly disturbed by such issues as Joseph Chamberlain's campaign for "fair trade," and, after 1906, by the Liberal Government's social legislation. Yet the King, who had inherited the throne at the height of its prestige, was able to provide, to a great extent by means of his remarkable personality, a kind of confidence and certainty that may have been superficial but nevertheless was vitally important to many of his subjects. Whatever troubles England might be suffering from, it could not be denied that its King was the first gentleman of Europe and one of the great personalities in the world. Who could doubt the continued primacy of England in the face of the undoubted primacy of its King? Who could doubt that all problems and challenges would be overcome as long as such a man as Edward VII was on the throne?

The life of the new King was thus surrounded by a great display of magnificence. This magnificence was perfectly suited to the new century, and contributed to a very important degree to the image of the King. It can be seen, therefore, that the spectacular revival of Court life is by no means of trivial significance. The splendor at court was for many people one of the most appealing things about the Edwardian monarchy, for it was the outward and visible manifestation of a break with the past, and of the new confidence that emanated from the throne. In spite of some minor relaxations in dress requirements for men, the Court radiated formality and glitter. At Windsor women were required to wear tiaras and men court dress with decorations every night. No woman was allowed to go to bed before the Queen, and no man before the King. Edward VII once went so far as to go around counting the men present, and when he discovered that one was missing he sent a page to bring back the absentee, who turned out to be the seventy-five-year-old Keeper of the Privy Purse, who had crept off to bed. Precedence and rank were, as one would suspect, at the center of Court life, even if it involved embarrassment for great powers. The

King insisted, for example, that King Kalakua of the Cannibal Islands take precedence over the Crown Prince of Germany. The Germans objected, but the King replied, "Either the brute is a King or else he is an ordinary black nigger, and if he is not a King, why is he here?"[24]

The new glitter of Court life probably ended by pleasing most of the upper class, who responded by imitating many royal mannerisms; those who could afford to do so repaid royal hospitality with an ostentation of their own. No longer did lavish entertainments earn disapproval from Windsor, Osborne, or Balmoral. Quite the contrary: the King, much to society's pleasure, was extremely fond of dining, or being otherwise amused, in the houses of his subjects. Tradesmen came to see the advantage of having a style-conscious King; the Court was now influential in the world of fashion, and royal taste in clothes, food, and wine was widely followed. Most important of all, however, was the new visibility of the sovereign. Parliament was now regularly opened in person by the King, a custom that has been followed ever since by his successors; Victoria had rarely done so. On Valentine's Day, less than a month after his mother's death, he drove to Parliament "in George III's state coach in a magnificent procession which was received by the London crowd, still sombre in black for the Queen, with rapture."[25] For Londoners this type of spectacle was new, and the King heightened the effect by having all the peers who possessed state coaches drive to Parliament in them.

Although Victoria had largely overcome, in part through sheer longevity, the unpopularity she had earned as the widow of Windsor, it is doubtful if her successors could have survived so easily wihout the "show" that has come to be associated with monarchy. The ordinary man in the street, the newspaper and magazine reading public, and, more recently, the millions watching television, are allowed to participate vicariously in the activities of the great and the powerful; they are able to see and to read about historical pageants of great drama and splendor which are intensely interesting. Royalty, always the center of attention in these pageants, was thus personalized and humanized, but never made ordinary or commonplace. Edward VII's understanding of the necessity for pomp is perhaps an aspect of his vulgarity, but it is also a sign of his instinctive comprehension of what so many common people wanted and needed in an age in which government and national life, like everything else, had become increasingly large and impersonal.

This can be seen in the appeal which Edward VII held for the lower classes. They liked the King, and were either unaware of or simply accepted his lack of interest in their plight. He did admittedly spend £30,000 to give a dinner for half a million London poor on his accession, but of far greater importance is the fact that Edward simply acted as they thought a King should act. They enjoyed betting on his horses, and when Minoru won the Derby in 1909

> a surge of elemental joy went out to greet the Sovereign whose ample frame and genial face embodied every human quality which his countrymen understood best and loved.

Tens of thousands of people sang "God Save the King" and cheered again and again. They indulged in a delirious abandon which relieves very occasionally the reserve to which most Englishmen become habituated; and even the stolid policemen who moved mechanically to surround the King when he left the royal box to lead in his horse, threw care to the winds, waved helmets in the air, and joined jockeys, peers, shopkeepers and touts in yelling, "Good old Teddy! Teddy boy! Hurrah! Hurrah!"[26]

Unlike his mother, who so appealed to the middle classes, he seemed intensely human because his grandeur was combined with an earthy appetite. Victoria's isolation probably did the monarchy more harm with the working classes than with any other group in society.[27]

Those people whom the Marxists like to call the "possessing class" also came to develop, for the most part, a strong attachment to their King. Even that part of the middle classes that had been most shocked by Edward VII's behavior as Prince of Wales because of the discredit which it brought upon the established institutions of the country were now prepared, simply out of respect for those very institutions, to bury the past; they took it for granted that, once on the throne, the new King would deserve the respect which no one would refuse the sovereign.[28] In fact, for everyone who had a stake in society, Edward VII quickly became a kind of magical figure who symbolized an unchanging universe, or what they wished were an unchanging universe. No matter what dreadful things might be happening on the surface, in Parliament, in the trade-unions, and abroad, the monarchy showed that, fundamentally, all was well. The rapid change in what today is called the King's "image" showed the great strain that was felt by many of his subjects during his reign. Even those who never overcame their dislike of the King felt in no position to poke publicly at the dike standing between them and the forces of revolution led by men like Lloyd George. The King's very existence was a comfort; a novelist has caught this feeling very well:

> [Lady Montdore's] quilt was covered with newspapers and opened letters and the *Times* neatly folded back at the Court Circular, probably the only part of it she ever looked at, since news, she used to say, can always be gleaned, and far more entertainingly too, from those who make it. I think she felt comfortable, rather like reading prayers, to begin the day with Mabell, Countess of Airlie having succeeded the Lady Elizabeth Motion as lady in waiting to the Queen. It indicated that the globe was still revolving in accordance with the laws of nature.[29]

The extraordinary way in which the King had come to be a kind of demi-god who was able to ward off bad spirits can be seen in the overpowering grief with which his death was greeted. Wilfred Blunt was not overstating the case when he wrote, at the time of the King's death, that "the absurdities written in every newspaper about him pass belief. He might have been a Solon and a Francis of Assisi combined if the characters drawn of him were true."[30] One little girl was told by her mother, "as you go through life . . . I want you always to remember King Edward and to be proud of having seen him at his funeral. It will give you richness of spirit and glamour."[31] Memoirs and autobiographies are full of the most maudlin descriptions of the sorrow that overwhelmed many English. Julian Grenfell wrote to his mother, Lady Desborough, who had been a close friend of the King's, that there was tragedy in the atmosphere, which one could see in the people's faces: "Everybody *is* looking quite different, and one can feel the thundercloud in the air."[32] Lord Suffield recalled that in "those first blank and terrible days life itself seemed to have come to an end for me; there was neither interest nor savour in anything, and it was as though some icy hand had gripped and frozen my heart."[33] Sonia Keppel, a daughter of the King's mistress, has described how "a pall of darkness hung over the house," and how her father explained to her that nothing "will ever be the same again," because "Kingy was such a wonderful man."[34] Not surprisingly the mourning for the King often assumed ludicrous proportions; one man in Jermyn Street filled his store window with black Bradenham hams, and one woman tied a black bow on a tree which Edward had planted five years before.[35] The "Black Ascot" of June 1910 was a spectacular sight, as the social and racing worlds flaunted their woe.[36]

But all this grief, genuine as it may have been, was to a great extent a cover for bitter political feelings. With the King gone, anything was now possible. Daisy Cornwallis-West, now the Princess of Pless, wrote to Asquith to let him know that she thought the King's death had been hastened by the crisis which he, as Prime Minister, was fomenting; this crisis, she recorded later, had been brought on by "the uprising of a fierce and vindictive spirit of Socialism," and by the "cynical attempts" of Edward's ministers to destroy the much-needed House of Lords. She could hardly bear the thought of ever returning to England.[37] Even Mrs. Asquith was greatly affected by the death of the King; she thought that a frightful and dangerous event had occurred.[38] Victoria Sackville-West caught the spirit of the times very well; as a character in one of her novels said, "with so much Socialism about, one doesn't know what may happen; and now the King is dead I expect it will get worse; I always felt he kept things together somehow."[39]

The King was thus rapidly enshrined in the minds of many of his fellow-countrymen. It is not in the least surprising, therefore, that the appearance in 1912 of Sir Sidney Lee's article on the King in the *Dictionary of National Biography* caused a considerable stir. Although Sir Sidney had simply written that Edward, whatever his other virtues, had been too lazy, intellectually and otherwise, to exercise much direct influence on British policy, a great number of people were utterly outraged. Sir Sidney's comments were seen as extraordinarily vicious and dangerous, for they attacked the man who had come to symbolize the essence of British civilization and all the highest values toward which it was possible to strive. As has been made clear above, criticism of royalty in general, and of Edward VII in particular, had been quite common in the nineteenth century, although it is true that the ascent of Victoria to heaven had begun well before her death. But the extraordinary reaction to Sir Sidney's article clearly showed that criticism of the sovereign was henceforth going to be considered, by a substantial portion of the nation, as close to disloyalty. This sanctification of royalty is, therefore, as much an Edwardian as a Victorian legacy; Edward VII, who in his youth and middle age had been attacked far more than was probably justified, was after his death idolized far more than was surely justified. But he deepened the hold of the monarchy by his appeal to many different segments of the nation, and because of the increasing tendency of many Englishmen to cling to the throne amid the dangers of the twentieth century. Little had this been foreseen by his nineteenth-century critics, including the critic-in-chief herself, Queen Victoria.[40]

Edward VII thus added important new elements to the legacy left by his mother. But what of the political role of the sovereign? Many of the King's contemporaries firmly believed that he exercised a profound influence on domestic and especially foreign affairs. Lord Esher, a confidant of several sovereigns who prided himself on his knowledge of the inner workings of British life, claimed that in foreign affairs the King's brilliance and insight had saved England from disaster.[41] Although the English press at the time of the King's death was balanced in its interpretation of his influence,[42] the story that Edward VII was a power in international affairs has been perpetuated by historians ever since.[43] Certainly foreign observers made impressive claims for the power of the King. A generally well-informed American, Price Collier, confidentially asserted that Edward VII was "more powerful than any man, any class, any sect, any minister, or either of the houses of Parliament."[44] A German saw the King as "the soul of British policy," and as "England's secret Emperor." It made no difference which party was in power, for "King Edward, who stands behind both, rules."[45] The German Emperor himself shared that point of view, and regarded his uncle as "the arch-intriguer and mischief-maker in Europe."[46] In France, the rightist leader, Charles Maurras, thought that King Edward, with his cigars and his dinners, controlled the parliamentary committees of France.[47] One story that illustrates particularly well this tendency to exaggerate the King's power was told by one of Prime Minister Sir Henry Campbell-Bannerman's secretaries. One day at Marienbad this secretary showed Campbell-Bannerman an illustrated paper with a sketch of the King talking very seriously, striking a hand in a palm, while the Prime Minister listened gravely. Around them visitors stood at a respectful distance. The picture bore the title, "Is it Peace or War?", and a note explained that Austrian opinion was excited over the meeting of high British political and military authorities with the ruler of Bulgaria; the question under discussion was believed to be whether Britain and Bulgaria would join hands in a Balkan war. But when Campbell-Bannerman looked at the paper, he said solemnly to his secretary, "Would you like to know what the King was saying to me? He wanted to have my opinion whether halibut is better baked or boiled."[48]

As this story indicates, the King's power was much less than it appeared. In fact, the reign of Edward VII marked an important decline in royal power. One of the reasons for this was the simple yet important fact that Edward VII was an exceedingly lazy man. In the modern world a sovereign who wishes to exercise influence must do his homework and spend vast amounts of time immersed in documents of great length and tedium. This, as was shown, was at the core of Victoria's influence; her example has been followed by George V, George VI, and Elizabeth II. But Edward VII did not like to be bored, even for a moment. Sir Frederick Ponsonby wrote that "It was with matters that did not interest him that he was at his worst, and would never make the slightest effort to go into the details of anything that bored him."[49] In spite of the growth of democracy, knowledge and prestige might have given him some influence—although it would have been slight at best—in domestic affairs; but the King was bored by them, and would rush through any papers relating to them.[50]

Even in foreign affairs, which did interest him, the King's knowledge and influence were superficial. His travels around Europe and his close blood ties with almost all of the sovereigns of Europe gave a veneer of plausibility to the assertion of an historian, writing a dozen years after the King's death, that Edward was "in the main his own Foreign Minister, initiating, commanding, and controlling all . . . policy towards other powers."[51] Yet the evidence seems strong that even in international affairs Edward VII contributed to the decline of royal influence simply because of his lack of ability to concentrate. Lord Newton, the biographer of Lord Lansdowne, the Foreign Secretary from 1900 to 1905, wrote that the conception of the King as "a tireless intriguer working for the encirclement of Germany is little less than an instance of international hallucination." Newton quotes Arthur Balfour, who said that he remembered no suggestion of any sort from the King on big questions of policy.[52] Lansdowne's successor as Foreign Secretary, Sir Edward Grey, later wrote that the King rarely made a comment of any significance on a despatch; Sir Edward, like Arthur Balfour, remembered no criticism or suggestion from the King, which, Grey went on to say, is not unusual when one considers that "he did not care for long and sustained discussions about large aspects of policy."[53]

There seems to be, in fact, little evidence to sustain Sir Frederick Ponsonby's assertion that the King read everything concerning foreign affairs with care;[54] recent research supports the position of Balfour and Grey that his views on international relations were trivial and superficial. They were, furthermore, often impetuous and inconsistent, even on major issues. He was easily influenced by personalities; his view of Anglo-German relations was determined largely by his feelings for his nephew, the Kaiser. In foreign affairs his principal influence was in the field of diplomatic appointments, as he was occasionally decisive in advancing the careers of his friends, and in ceremonial matters, over which he exercised great influence.[55] As Frank Hardie points out, the King enjoyed the pageantry, not the politics, of diplomacy. He was "neither statesman nor diplomatist. He lacked the former's ability to conceive a policy, the latter's patience in implementing one. He was a salesman of foreign policy."[56] It is probable that all of the King's energy was expended on the fringes of foreign affairs. There he could be of some real use. As "he was by far the biggest and most striking personality in Europe,"[57] and as he was "a living encyclopedia of information concerning the tastes and habits of monarchs, diplomatists, and politicians, and of the more ambiguous people who pulled the strings in the world's capitals," he was definitely "a sensitive instrument of statecraft even if he was not a statesman."[58] Sir Edward Grey recognized this and did not hesitate to give the King credit for being an "immense advantage" to the state.[59]

This "immense advantage" was seen most effectively during Edward's triumphal visit to Paris in 1903. There can be no question that the King played a significant part in making the entente with France possible from a public relations point of view; the mistake of many observers was in believing that he played a role in formulating the policy for which he smoothed the path. Nevertheless, the success of the visit ought not to be underestimated. As the Belgian representative in Paris said,

> His Majesty has been completely successful. Not a word, not an action which was not appropriate to the circumstances and the persons. It is said that Edward VII has won the hearts of all the French. Seldom has such a complete change of attitude been seen as that which has taken place in the last fortnight towards England and her sovereign.[60]

The King's overpowering charm and his obvious love for France triumphed over all obstacles. "Vivent les Boers," "Vive Fashoda," and even "Vive Jeanne d'Arc," soon gave way to widely enthusiastic crowds greeting the sovereign with thunderous applause, and to incessant shouts of "Vive Edouard" and "Notre bon Edouard."[61] The magic which the British monarchy holds for foreigners as well as for its own subjects has never been so well demonstrated.

Edward VII, therefore, removed the monarchy farther from a central role in politics. Far more than was the case with his mother, who was more intelligent, Edward VII thought of politics as the extension of personality; he seemingly had little sense of policies and programs. Although he was probably as much a Tory as he was anything, he did not have the deep political antipathies of his mother. Much as Victoria detested Gladstone, it is certain that the basis of her dislike was a dislike of his policies. Edward VII liked and loathed far more on a superficial personal level. Therefore he lacked the will, as well as the energy, to pursue a certain course. As a result he suffered, at the hands of a Conservative Government, a series of rebuffs which, although usually minor, were humiliating.[62] The King, moreover, did not have the room for maneuver which his mother had possessed; "more and more . . . the relations between the Sovereign and the Government were not between him and Ministers, at the formative stage of policy-making, but between him and the Prime Minister, acting as spokesman of a Cabinet which had already made up its mind."[63] At any rate, it is clear that the Tories showed no particular consideration for the King's prerogatives; the Liberals, in fact, were more willing to defer to his *amour propre* than the Conservatives.[64]

Yet is must also be emphasized that Edward VII's wishes, questions, and whims were by no means insignificant matters for those involved in the actual government of the country. Supposedly cabinet ministers, generals, and admirals would "absolutely curl up in his presence when trying to maintain their point."[65] His displeasure was by no means a minor matter to a minister or a civil servant, and the King's ability to make his likes and dislikes known in a great number of influential circles was more than enough to make powerful men think carefully before opposing him. In part because of this, the King did exercise considerable influence in some areas, in the army and the navy, for example. It is the consensus that, without the support of the King, Sir John Fisher's naval reforms would not have prevailed; the leading authority on the British navy at this time, Arthur Marder, shares this opinion, and Frank Hardie states that the King's support of naval reform was the greatest single achievement of his reign.[66] In military affairs his support of Haldane was crucial in bringing about the restructuring of the British army.[67] Clearly, his role in military and naval affairs was greater and more beneficial than his role in diplomacy.

There is no doubt that Edward VII's minor role in the government of England was fortunate, both for the country and for the monarchy itself. The views of the King, if they could be called views at all, hardly qualified him as a modern political leader. He had the ease, charm, and sophistication of his friends, but also their narrowness. Lady Warwick, an extremely close friend of the King's who later horrified him by adopting radical views, pointed out that the Marlborough House set did not like brains:

> We acknowledged that it was necessary that pictures should be painted, books written, the law administered; we even acknowledged that there was a certain class whose job it might be to do these things. But we did not see why their achievements entitled them to our recognition; they might disturb, overstimulate, or even bore. On rare occasions, if a book made a sufficient stir, we might read it, or better still, get somebody to tell us about it, and so save us the trouble. . . . The chief folly of those of us who belonged to the Marlborough House Set was to imagine that pleasure and happiness were identical.[68]

The King thus disliked "intellectuals," such as Arthur Balfour, his Prime Minister from 1902 to 1905. For Edward and his clique, "clever men are 'prigs'; clever women 'too advanced'; Liberals are 'Socialists'; the uninteresting 'pleasant'; the interesting 'intriguers'; and the dreamer 'mad.'"[69] He had no idea of the great changes taking place in his country, and continued to regard the world as an appendage to his own family affairs, often with appalling results. For example, the King and Queen were planning to go to

Russia in 1908, to visit the King's niece, the Czarina, and the Queen's nephew, the Czar. It was to be a state visit, carried out on the Government's advice. The Labour Party reacted strongly, and Ramsay MacDonald, in *Labour Leader*, called the Czar a common murderer, and objected to the King hobnobbing with "a bloodstained creature." Keir Hardie thought that the visit would condone the Czar's atrocities. The King, instead of retiring behind his Government's advice, took the attack as a personal affront on himself and his family; as Sir Sidney Lee put it, the unrest in Russia did not concern him and "only awoke in him sympathy for the ruler whose life it oppressed."[70] As punishment for voting in favor of a motion aimed against the visit, Edward struck the names of Arthur Ponsonby, Keir Hardie, and Victor Grayson off the guest list for a garden party at Windsor Castle. After Ponsonby decided that this act amounted to political pressure, the issue was taken up by the press and Edward found himself in a ridiculous position. He then agreed to invite Hardie and Grayson on future occasions, but not Ponsonby; his crime was far worse than that of the others, for he had been well-born and should have known better—after all, his father had been Queen Victoria's private secretary. Only the intervention of third parties and an apology persuaded the King to restore Ponsonby's name to the royal guest list.[71] This event shows clearly Edward's lack of comprehension of the modern world, especially his inability to understand that political issues could exist independently of him and his family. His lack of power to intervene effectively in politics was obviously one of his and the monarchy's greatest protections.

Nevertheless, it was the personality of Edward VII which breathed new life into the monarchy. He was less powerful than his mother, but he did symbolize power to much greater advantage than she.[72] His combination of "bonhomie and dignity,"[73] his ability to cover ignorance and boredom by seemingly attentive listening,[74] his passion for splendor, and his great charm disarmed the skeptical and won him a popularity that exceeded in potency the rather abstract awe in which Victoria was held. A man who spoke English with a German accent, he became the quintessence of Englishness, and his "guttural compliments" became the highest accolade in the country.[75] He made it easier for people to identify with the royal family, but he avoided bringing royalty down to a banal level where it would lose all its glamour and interest. And certainly the King's conspicuous enjoyment of kingship contributed greatly to his success, and made him a most appealing figure.[76]

Furthermore, his laziness prevented the clashes that might have occurred had a brighter and more energetic monarch been on the throne. The decline in royal prerogative, which has so well shielded the throne from political controversy in the twentieth century, took place largely unnoticed, covered by the barrage of magnificence sent up from Buckingham Palace, Windsor, Sandringham, and Balmoral after 1901. But if his reign destroyed virtually all of the vestiges of royal power and undermined most of the bases of direct royal influence, the monarchy's ability to influence politics subtly and indirectly remained; a dutiful, hardworking "Victorian" King, as subsequent chapters will show, would be able to bring his prestige and his knowledge to bear in a most effective manner. It was quickly realized that Edward VII's power had been grossly overestimated; the mistake has since been made of grossly underestimating the influence of his successors. During Edward's reign royal influence was more apparent than real; since his death it has generally been more real than apparent. A better formula for modern monarchy could not be devised.

The contributions of Victoria and Albert to the modern monarchy were essential; they made it respectable and identified it with the nation as a whole. They took the first and most important steps away from overt political partisanship. But this was not enough. Edward VII was needed to make the monarchy fascinating and to give it the splendor so increasingly necessary in modern Britain, where splendor did not come as easily as before. It is unlikely, however, that the rather vulgar, excessive and indulgent atmosphere of Edwardian magnificence would have had much appeal after the horrors of the First World War. Some kind of synthesis was needed in which the magnificence would be maintained, but wrapped in an aura of Victorian duty and respectability and presided over by a man whose character and dedication would give him unassailable prestige. George V provided such a synthesis, which combined the best of the Victorian and Edwardian legacies, and formed the modern monarchy.

[1] Philip Magnus, *King Edward VII*, p. 3.
[2] Lytton Strachey, *Queen Victoria*, (London, 1948) p. 155.
[3] *The Letters of Queen Victoria*, first series, I, 365.
[4] Sir Sidney Lee, "King Edward VII," *Dictionary of National Biography*, second supplement, I, 547.
[5] Quoted Sir Sidney Lee, *King Edward VII*, I, 163–64.
[6] *The Letters of Queen Victoria*, second series, II, 19.
[7] Quoted in Arthur Ponsonby, *Henry Ponsonby*, p. 102.
[8] *Ibid.*, pp. 100–01.
[9] Philip Magnus, *King Edward VII*, pp. 179–80.
[10] Arthur Ponsonby, *Henry Ponsonby*, p. 109.
[11] An excellent and sympathetic biography of Queen Alexandra is Georgina Battiscombe, *Queen Alexandra*.
[12] See Philip Magnus, *King Edward VII*, chapters 6, 8, 12; Compton Mackenzie, *The Windsor Tapestry*, pp. 26–27; and George Dangerfield, *Victoria's Heir*, pp. 305–06.
[13] George Dangerfield, *Victoria's Heir*, p. 5. See also Consuelo Vanderbilt Balsan, *The Glitter and the Gold* (New York 1952), chapters 4, 5, and 6; Christopher Sykes, *Four Studies in Loyalty*, pp. 14ff; Virginia Cowles, *Gay Monarch* (New York 1956), pp. 157–58; and Christopher Hibbert, *The Court at Windsor*, p. 242.
[14] Quoted in Ursula Bloom, *The Elegant Edwardian*, pp. 21–22.
[15] Osbert Lancaster, *All Done From Memory*, p. 9.
[16] George Dangerfield, *Victoria's Heir*, p. 7.
[17] H. E. Wortham, *Edward VII*, p. 16.
[18] Sir Frederick Ponsonby, *Recollections of Three Reigns*, pp. 181ff.
[19] The Duke of Windsor, *A King's Story*, p. 47.
[20] T. H. White, *Farewell Victoria*, pp. 92, 94.
[21] Sir Sidney Lee, *King Edward VII*, II, 3.
[22] Kingsley Martin, *The Magic of Monarchy*, p. 19.
[23] George Dangerfield, *Victoria's Heir*, pp. 5–6.
[24] Sir Frederick Ponsonby, *Recollections of Three Reigns*, pp. 288–89; Christopher Hibbert, *The Court at Windsor*, pp. 242ff.
[25] Roger Fulford, *Hanover to Windsor*, p. 154.
[26] Philip Magnus, *King Edward VII*, p. 429. The King was extremely succesful with his horses. From 1886 to his death in 1910 they earned him £ 269,495 in stud fees, and £146,345 in stake money. *Ibid.*, p. 254.

[27] J. L. Garvin, *The Life of Joseph Chamberlain*, I, 152. See also E. H. Turner, *The Court of St. James's*, pp. 348–49.

[28] Elie Halevy, *A History of the English People in the Nineteenth Century*, V, 120.

[29] Nancy Mitford, *Love in a Cold Climate* (London 1949), p. 67. Although Miss Mitford was writing of a slightly later period, she perfectly expresses the outlook of many Edwardians.

[30] Wilfrid Scawen Blunt, *My Diaries*, II, 307.

[31] Quoted in Claire Leighton, *Tempestuous Petticoat: The Story of an Invincible Edwardian*, p. 34.

[32] Ethel Anne Priscilla Grenfell, Lady Desborough, *Pages From a Family Journal*, p. 183.

[33] Lord Suffield, *My Memories*, p. 355.

[34] Sonia Keppel, *Edwardian Daughter*, pp. 43–54.

[35] Lady Maud Warrender, *My First Sixty Years*, p. 79.

[36] One of the best accounts of "Black Ascot" is Cecil Beaton, *The Glass of Fashion* (London 1954), pp. 63–64.

[37] Princess of Pless, *Daisy, Princess of Pless*, pp. 211–12.

[38] Margot Asquith, *An Autobiography* (New York 1922), III, 200–01.

[39] Victoria Sackville-West, *The Edwardians* (Grosset & Dunlap ed.), p. 277.

[40] The best examples of the bitter reaction to Sir Sidney Lee are three books written to defend the King by Edward Legge: *King Edward in His True Colours* (1912); *More About King Edward* (1913); and *King Edward and The War* (1917). Sir Sidney was attacked strongly in 1956 in a popular and highly sympathetic biography of the King: Virginia Cowles, *Gay Monarch*, pp. 360ff.

[41] Lord Esher, "King Edward and Foreign Affairs," in Lord Esher, editor, *The Influence of King Edward*, pp. 49–60.

[42] See, for example, the *Times*, May 7, 1910; *The Economist*, LXX (1910), pp. 1062, 1118; *The Spectator*, May 14, 1910; *The Saturday Review*, CLXXXVII (1910), pp. 766–67.

[43] See, for instance, J. A. R. Marriott, *Modern England*, p. 298; and Luigi Albertini, *The Origins of the War of 1914*, I, 146.

[44] Price Collier, *England and the English*, p. 85.

[45] Rudolf Martin, *Kaiser Wilhelm und Eduard VII*, p. 31.

[46] See Michael Balfour, *The Kaiser and His Times*, p. 265.

[47] See Michael Curtis, *Three Against the Third Republic*, p. 202.

[48] J. A. Spender, *The Life of Sir Henry Campbell Bannerman*, II, 54–55.

[49] Sir Frederick Ponsonby, *Recollections of Three Reigns*, p. 385.

[50] *Ibid.*

[51] J. A. Farrar, *England Under Edward VII*, p. 5.

[52] Lord Newton, *Lord Lansdowne*, pp. 292–93.

[53] Viscount Grey of Fallodon, *Twenty-Five Years*, I, 197–98.

[54] Sir Frederick Ponsonby, *Recollections of Three Reigns*, p. 385.

[55] Zara Steiner, *The Foreign Office and Foreign Policy, 1898–1914*, p. 203, and *passim*.

[56] Frank Hardie, *The Political Influence of the British Monarchy*, pp. 101–03.

[57] Sir Frederick Ponsonby, *Recollections of Three Reigns*, p. 386.

[58] George Dangerfield, *Victoria's Heir*, p. 7.

[59] Viscount Grey of Fallodon, *Twenty-Five Years*, I, 200.

[60] Quoted in Sir Sidney Lee, *King Edward VII*, II, 241.

[61] Philip Magnus, *King Edward VII*, pp. 311–13.

[62] See Frank Hardie, *The Political Influence of the British Monarchy*, pp. 101–03.

[63] *Ibid.*, p. 90.

[64] Sir Sidney Lee, *King Edward VII*, II, 448.

[65] Sir Frederick Ponsonby, *Recollections of Three Reigns*, p. 386.

[66] Arthur Marder, *From the Dreadnought to Scapa Flow*, I, 100; Frank Hardie, *The Political Influence of the British Monarchy*, p. 98. See also Philip Magnus, *King Edward VII*, p. 277.

[67] See Roger Fulford, "The King," in Simon Nowell-Smith, ed., *Edwardian England, 1901–1914*, p. 25; and Stephen Koss, *Lord Haldane*, p. 45.

[68] Frances, Countess of Warwick, *Afterthoughts*, pp. 40–42.

[69] Margot Asquith, *An Autobiography*, III, 163.

[70] Sir Sidney Lee, *King Edward VII*, II, 588.

[71] See Philip Magnus, *King Edward VII*, pp. 404–06.

[72] See R. C. B. Ensor, *England 1870–1914*, p. 342.

[73] Viscount Grey of Fallodon, *Twenty-Five Years*, I, 199.

[74] Sir Frederick Ponsonby, *Recollections of Three Reigns*, p. 383.

[75] See Max Beerbohm's novel, *Zuleika Dobson*, Modern Library Edition, p. 22.

[76] J. B. Priestley, *The Edwardians*, p. 28.

CHAPTER 3

THE GEORGIAN SYNTHESIS: THE EMERGENCE OF THE MODERN MONARCHY

*D*uring the reign of George V most European monarchies, many of them rooted for centuries, were eclipsed by a republican tide. In 1910 the German Emperor, eight Kings and five Crown Princes attended the funeral of Edward VII as representatives of the monarchial guild. At the end of the next reign, in 1936, only a handful of those dynasties were still afloat. "During that quarter of a century," says Harold Nicolson, "the world witnessed the disappearance of five Emperors, eight Kings and eighteen minor dynasties."[1] This was, in the phrase of Sebastian Haffner, one of the "most spectacular political landslides"[2] in history.

By 1950 only monarchies on the periphery of the continent survived—Greece, Belgium, the Netherlands, the grand Duchy of Luxembourg, Great Britain, Denmark, Norway and Sweden. Except for Greece all were located in northern and western Europe. Spain was a monarchy in name only.[3]

Paradoxically republicans in Great Britain received little comfort from the success of their counterparts elsewhere. Their monarchy emerged from the political storm more firmly established than ever. It faced no republican party, and the republican movement, once so optimistic of success, had become "a narrow and eccentric sect."[4] The British royal family had also gained an "immeasurable prestige and grip on the national imagination"[5] which was to remain undiminished. Britons even took pride in the isolation of their royalty, and the snapping of links, so diligently fostered by Victoria, with innumerable European dynasties and duchies. This was symbolized in 1917 by the adoption of the very English name of Windsor for the royal family. Britain echoed the satisfaction expressed by Lord Macaulay in 1848 when the country was almost alone in escaping another wave of political convulsions:

> All around us the world is convulsed by the agonies of great nations.
> Governments which lately seemed likely to stand during ages have

been on a sudden shaken and overthrown. . . . Meanwhile in our island the regular course of government has never been for a day interrupted. . . . We have order in the midst of anarchy.[6]

What is the explanation for the continued stability of the monarchial tradition in Great Britain? Why the unprecedented upsurge of monarchial feeling during the reign of George V?

In explaining the durability of the British model political historians have emphasized one of the themes developed in this volume: the long Fabian retreat of the monarchy from political power, although not its forms. Traditional monarchs on the continent clung to the realities of political power but they paid the penalty for its misuse. The Spanish monarchy never recovered from its patronage of Primo de Rivera's dictatorship in the 1920s or the Italian from its association with Mussolini after 1922. Britain was frequently dismissed as a "crowned republic," but its monarchs, by their powerlessness, escaped identification with one political party, or with unpopular policies and discredited regimes. George V, although a crusty Tory, even presided over Socialist Governments in 1924 and 1929–31.

Strategic retreat on the political front left the British monarch less exposed than others. But the fragility or toughness of an object under attack is only one consideration: The strength of the blow also must be measured. Certainly continental monarchies faced far stiffer challenges than those encountered in Great Britain. Germany, Austria-Hungary, Russia and the Ottoman Empire faced the test of war between 1914 and 1918 and their royal dynasties became victims of domestic upheavals following on the heels of military defeat. Would national disaster have held a similar fate for the English monarchy? Perceptive observers around the throne feared so. Lord Esher wrote the King's private secretary on August 24, 1917:

If we really defeat the enemy England will recover her balance quickly enough. If we fail to beat the enemy and have to accept a compromise peace, then we shall be lucky if we escape a revolution in which the Monarchy, the Church and all our 'Victorian' institutions will founder . . . the institutions under which a war such as this was possible whether monarchial, parliamentary or diplomatic, will go under. I have met no one who, speaking his inmost mind, differs from this conclusion.[7]

Britain was spared the corrosive bitterness of defeat and its monarch became the "hierophant of victory,"[8] not an exposed social mummy. He became not a scapegoat, but a minor deity. With the signing of the armistice on the morning of November 11, 1918, large crowds in London spontaneously drifted to Buckingham to cheer the triumph of national qualities personified by the royal figure on the palace balcony.

Nor did Britain face an uncontrollable impulse for radical domestic change. Social stability, resting on an expanding democracy, was a common feature of all surviving monarchies of northern and western Europe. Argument and conflict sometimes reached a high pitch, especially in the economic and industrial spheres, but they did not result in revolutionary fervor. Class struggle was great in Britain between the wars and conflict was embittered by the General Strike in 1926 and a prolonged depression. But the parliamentary system was able to express divergent outlooks and absorb the Labour party and its demands for social democracy.

Such epochs of social conflict always pose at least a potential threat to monarchy. It must symbolize continuity and shared values at a time when the community is most divided about the qualities it admires. If disillusionment with existing norms runs deep, and reformers despair of change, monarchy may become identified with the nation to be torn down. William IV felt his Crown totter in 1832, but the Reform Bill in that year, followed by a series of others in 1867, 1884 and 1911, kept the average citizen within hailing distance of political equality and the country on the right side of revolution. In the twentieth century social reform measures, sponsored by all political parties and culminating in the welfare state after 1945, served the same purpose. As Lord David Cecil observed:

> The average citizen must be pleased with his present if he is to be loyal to his past as embodied in an ancient institution like the king.[9]

At times of greatest social unanimity—such as the late 1940s and early 1950s, when all political parties occupied the common ground of the welfare state and managed economy—the monarchy faces little criticism. In the parliamentary debate on the Civil List in 1952 even the handful of professional republicans in the House of Commons was lethargic. It was the quietest debate on the Civil List in history, according to a Conservative Member, because there was little difference between the two sides.[10]

But the Crown has, in fact, been much more than a useful political symbol to many in the United Kingdom. Otherwise it is doubtful whether it could have survived; certainly it would not have become so rooted in the affection of the public. Apparently George V was a particularly reassuring father figure in an anxious age between the two wars. And while the cult of the strong man grew on the continent, monarchy in Britain apparently satisfied a natural craving for ritual and for heroes larger than life.

As a result it is possible that the Crown, although an impotent authority, was a potent factor in stabilizing Parliamentary government between the wars. The monarchy may have reduced personal and governmental unease created by the rise of dictators in Europe and by the political tensions within the party system in Great Britain. This was the judgment of Dr. Ernest Jones, a Freudian psychologist, which he argued in a provocative article* published in 1936.

---

*See Appendix A.

According to Jones, man has an ambivalent attitude toward authority, from which the basic problem of government arises. He feels the need of authority to control his impulses; but when restrictions are imposed upon him, he immediately clamors for freedom. Authority, in the form of rulers, therefore provokes feelings of either hatred or love, depending on the prevailing need. When hatred is directed against authority it becomes a destructive impulse which leads to "revolution which may attain a murderous intensity."

In constitutional monarchy, however, the ruler is segregated into two persons, one "untouchable, irremovable and sacrosanct, above even criticism, let alone attack; the other vulnerable in such a degree that sooner or later he will be destroyed, i.e. expelled from his position of power."[11] As a protective and benevolent figure, one without power to harm, the constitutional monarch becomes a satisfying form of political authority. The governed may be out of sympathy with his elected and powerful representatives, but monarchy remains a reassuring source of the individual's identification with the community. It is the Prime Minister who suffers the destructive impulse. He becomes, in the phrase of David Frost and Anthony Jay, a "mock-king, a joke-hero, chosen by the tribe to be feted for a brief while and then destroyed."[12] He must atone for the deepest feelings of guilt or hatred in the community.

Constitutional monarchy is therefore a useful device for resolving mutually antagonistic impulses residing in every man. In the process society is fortified and the vigor of political life is rendered possible, according to sociologists Edward Shils and Michael Young, because aggressiveness in the political arena is softened. Love "directed towards a genuinely love-worthy object, reduces the intensity of the hatred as well."[13]

This thesis was not left unchallenged, but it found favor with many political scientists, was translated into other terms and was reproduced in one variation or another in many studies of the British political system. The British act "with sober pragmatism in parliamentary politics," says the political scientist Harry Eckstein, "because their political passions are channelled towards and satisfied by other aspects of the political system; their ceremonial institutions—above all, of course, the monarchy."[14] The "dualistic orientation" towards political authority in Great Britain, writes Eric A. Nordlinger, has guaranteed the absence of an "excessively emotion-laden politics" and permitted a set of "pragmatic attachments" to substantive issues.[15]

A heavy accent upon ceremonial institutions may also suggest a special capacity for escapism and nostalgia which discourages progress by reinforcing a preference for the status quo. But Britain nourished a stable and reasonably humane democracy between the wars, and it is possible, as Ernest Jones argued, that the monarchy played a significant role in that achievement.

The popularity of the Georgian monarchy also rested upon the character of the King and of his consort, Queen Mary. The strengthening of the monarchy between 1910 and 1936, "a fact contrary to the whole tendency of the age," Winston Churchill has written, "cannot be separated from the personality of the good, wise and truly noble King" who reigned during those years.[16] George V fulfilled so admirably the various functions expected of a constitutional monarch—dignified head of government, benevolent father-figure, and ideal of his people—that he increased the appeal of the institution.

This outcome was not anticipated at the beginning of the new reign. George V lacked his father's public presence and "the smile that includes crowds"; he adopted "a less expansive dignity," marked by a touch of doggedness, and this produced an impression of solidness.[17] Smart society also mocked the "decorous domesticity and serious manner" of the new Court.[18] But solidness and seriousness at Court apparently satisfied a public need; monarchy became a reassuring symbol of stability in an age of swift and often frightening change.

Labour circles in particular welcomed the new style of kingship. Nonconformity, a powerful force in shaping Labour opinion, found George V more praiseworthy as a person than Edward VII, and his Court less extravagant. Monarchy was no longer linked with exclusive "society."[19] This more cordial response to monarchy on the part of Labour was extremely important, because it was under George V that the country had its first Labour Government, when J. Ramsay MacDonald kissed the royal hand in 1924 and became Britain's first Socialist Prime Minister.

Labour ministers at Buckingham Palace were a clear sign of a tremendous shift of power in the British constitution, the dimensions of which the King could appreciate by reflecting on the steady increase in Party and trade union membership. In 1910 the Labour Party claimed 1,431,000 members. By 1919 the figures had risen to over 3 million and by 1920 had reached 4,360,000. Trade union membership, the chief manpower and financial source for the Party, showed a similar upward trend. In 1910 trade unions recorded 2,477,000 members, in 1918 some 5,499,000 and by 1921 over 8 million.[20] That trade union power, when mobilized for political purposes, played a leading role in casting the Liberals into the shadows and projecting Labour into power as a minority government in 1924 and 1929.

This transformation raised a number of questions for monarchy. Victoria had said she could not and would not be the Queen of a "democratic monarchy." How would her grandson respond to the effects of democracy? Would he act as a "Socialist King"? Would he have the confidence of his Socialist ministers? And what of the party? Would it demand a modification in the institution of monarchy? How, in fact, did Labour reconcile monarchy with its vision of a Socialist Commonwealth based on social equality?

Several personal gestures of George V in 1924 suggest how eager he was to accommodate Labour and prove that democracy and kingship were not incompatible. Apparently he wore a red tie for the first audience given to MacDonald;[21] toward his new ministers he was "kindness and sympathy itself."[22] The Labour leaders responded in a similar manner; to the dismay of austere Socialists they even agreed to follow traditional practice regarding ceremonial occasions and court dress. The King, who was devoted to established protocol, did not insist on the traditional knee-breeches but sent word to his new Ministers that they might hire "a few suits of Household Second Class Levée Dress" from Moss Brothers, a celebrated firm which rented clothes to fit all occasions. The Labour leaders, instead of taking offense, thanked the King for his kindness and sympathy.[23] Although a fervent republican early in his career, Ramsay MacDonald appreciated the goodwill of George V, and came to respect his counsel. In 1931, in fact, MacDonald's colleagues complained of his readiness to follow royal advice before their own.

The success of the King with his Socialist Ministers was all the more remarkable because he was "an absolutely dyed-in-the-wool conservative" himself. Years after George V's death J. C. C. Davidson, a prominent Conservative politician, observed: "He was very right-wing and he knew where his friends really lay, and that the Conservative Party was the King's Party and a radical party was not. But he managed to persuade the Labour Party that he was entirely neutral. That must have required a great deal of self-discipline."[24]

The monarchy also acknowledged the need to adapt to the new political facts by making a conscious effort to broaden its symbolism. Members of the royal family began to extend the range of their activities by visiting industrial sections of the country and putting royal approval on humble and useful services. In the 4 years before 1914 the royal family did not visit more than 20 factories[25] but the war effort and an era of industrial strife heightened this aspect of the dignified role of monarchy as the royal family made a determined effort to move among the working classes. While the Prince of Wales acted as royalty's chief goodwill ambassador to Empire, the Duke of York was largely responsible for performing the same duties on the domestic front. On his tours he appeared not only as a Prince of the royal blood, but also as the President of the Industrial Welfare Society, a private association with the dual object of improving conditions within factories, and enriching life outside the shop and mine through a variety of educational and recreational projects.[26] By visiting factories, climbing down coal shafts and moving among workers, the Duke earned the epithet of "the Industrial Prince."

Amid industrial strife the Duke of York offered his own experiment for sweetening industrial relations and encouraging greater social harmony. He patronized a summer camp for the mixing of public school students and working boys at which they were expected as Engishmen to triumph over class differences. The experiment was conducted on a small scale, and was rather contrived, but the camps were a useful index of the new behavior pattern of monarchy. As long as monarchy performed so adequately republicanism was not likely to make headway in Britain.

Republicanism, in fact, never became a serious proposition and the Labour party was never tempted to touch the issue. J. H. Thomas, Colonial Secretary in the first Labour Government, contended in 1920 that the party had heated controversies on almost every subject, but "no question of Republicanism as a serious proposition" ever found a place in Labour discussions.[27] A private resolution stating "That the Royal Family is no longer necessary as part of the British Constitution" was placed before the Annual Party Conference in 1923 but defeated overwhelmingly, 3,694,000 votes against 386,000.[28] Such resolutions only embarrassed party leaders; once in office not a single minister remained openly republican. In 1937 the Party Leader, Clement Attlee, said flatly: "We accept the constitutional Monarchy as we have it in this country."[29]

Attlee and Thomas were the voice of the moderates in a party largely peopled by moderates. The accommodation with monarchy, however, did arouse the anger of the ardent Socialists in the Labour movement. They were convinced that acceptance of the traditional forms of society weakened the party's resolve in attacking traditional values. The court dress affair of 1924 thus loomed in their minds as the beginning of the rot; it signified the failure of a Labour Government to appreciate the importance of social equality. Kingsley Martin argues this view in his *The Crown and the Establishment*. Even working-class members of the new Government are seen as delighting in the dress of their aristocratic predecessors. Such an attitude, says Martin, foreshadowed the "betrayal" of 1931 when MacDonald and his cronies turned against their former party and became a part of the establishment.[30]

These Socialist critics ascribed the intensification of loyalty for monarchy in the twentieth century to a skillful campaign waged by the vested interests as a means of fostering respect for the "scales of privilege." Propaganda on monarchy was pumped into people from birth; royalty made its appearance in nursery rhymes and in *Alice in Wonderland*. Superstitious loyalty was also encouraged by public prayers and festive ceremonies, royal portraits and royal tours, loyal toasts and the National Anthem. Monarchy had no special mystique; its popularity was rooted in guided and learned responses.[31]

It is doubtful, however, if such party worthies as Sidney and Beatrice Webb, Stafford Cripps, Hugh Dalton and Clement Attlee were seduced by the propaganda of the vested interests. They were practical politicians who recognized the strength of monarchical sentiment and trimmed their sails accordingly. As a small pressure group the Party could afford to promote unfashionable ideas but as a major political movement it needed to broaden its base of support, appear more respectable and blunt Conservative gibes that it was unfit to rule. With power within its grasp the Party was not inclined to embrace so quixotic an issue as republicanism.[32]

The positive approach to monarchy, however, was also the outcome of the Party's devotion to "gradualness," to the democratic method, and to the stability of parliamentary government.

Before the First World War the Labour Party acted primarily as a pressure group for organized labor in the House of Commons. Although a member of the Second International, the Party cooperated with the Liberals, and its thought and values could be fitted into the ideology of Liberal Radicalism. Its leaders were largely indifferent to socialist theory. "Marxist ideas just did not get through to them," Ivan Maisky, a future Russian ambassador, observed in 1913.[33]

In 1918, the party undertook a definite shift in ideology. It adopted a new constitution written by Sidney Webb and committed itself for the first time to a Socialist basis. Discontent now centered on the capitalist economic system; the only solution to social ills, read the celebrated Clause Four of the constitution, was "the common ownership of the means of production and the best obtainable system of popular administration and control of each industry or service."[34] Now Labour sought political power in order to abolish the capitalist system and not, as before, only to make it more humane by radical reform. Lloyd George perceived the change when he remarked that "In the old days when there was discontent, you could blame your parties for it, but now you have to blame systems, and that is the danger."[35]

The shift to the left, however, did not alter the Party's attitude toward parliamentary democracy. It remained "massively devoted to parliamentary and democratic methods." It would accomplish its aims "statute by statute."[36] This commitment to gradualism earned the contempt of continental Marxists. Maisky found British labor a "Giant in Chains" because it always adhered to legalism in everything and anything. The philosophy of gradualism, he wrote, kept the proletariat "entangled in strong internal fetters" and thus its conscience and will "in bourgeois captivity."[37] But Maisky also includes in his memoirs the answer of a British Socialist:

> We're a democracy, and you are a tsarist autocracy. You Russians may have other methods; it takes us English a long time to win our rights but we win them for good. We don't need revolutions; we have Parliament. We shall get socialism that way.[38]

This steadfast constitutionalism affected the Party's view of monarchy, as Maisky was quick to notice. As an example of the muddleheadedness of his English colleagues he reproduces in his memoirs a conversation he heard at a Socialist vacation camp in 1913:

> 'And when we have established socialism [announced a socialist speaker] there will be no need to change the existing form of government.' Someone in the audience called out: 'Are we going to keep the King?' 'Of course we are,' was the emphatic answer. 'In England the King does what the people want. He will be a socialist King.'[39]

To Maisky such sentiment was additional proof of those chains binding Labour to the will of the establishment. But British Labour leaders, in recognizing the Crown, were fully aware of the implications of parliamentary democracy. As a Party liable to possess a parliamentary majority and to form a government, it needed to act in such a manner as to claim the same legal and moral acceptance for its acts as other parties and governments claimed for theirs. It would wish to invoke the traditional allegiance of the civil service and the armed services, and at least the tolerance of the whole community. Perhaps more than others, therefore, a Socialist Government would find monarchy useful, as Michael Stewart, a moderate leader of the Party, explained in 1952:

> The proposition that all citizens have a loyalty to the community which modifies partisan activity is essential to democracy; and any party in a democracy which aspires to government is ill advised to dispute a principle which it will later wish to invoke. In Britain, respect for the Crown is the accepted method of crystallising this loyalty; anyone who challenges the lawful authority of the elected Government risks the charge of disloyalty to his Sovereign. In this way a democratic principle is based not only on political theory but on strong and traditional emotions. Acceptance of the democratic method had led the Labour Party to a positive acceptance of monarchy; and the desire to make great economic changes made it all the more prudent to assert the lawful authority of any Government with Parliamentary majority.[40]

Stewart's optimistic analysis of an existing framework of consent within which all governments operate was written after Labour had ushered in a "cautious revolution" without provoking sharp social conflict. In the twenties and thirties the outcome had been less certian, and Harold Laski, a left-wing party intellectual, had predicted that a sustained clash between Socialism and capitalism would shatter the two-party system.[41] By 1952, however, the weight of evidence disproved his thesis. Labour conceded monarchy a useful role in the outcome: It had eased strains inherent in the democratic process of choosing and rejecting governments, and it commanded respect for a social revolution engineered by Labour but announced in the name of the Crown.

The experience of the thirties also led Labour to accept the social value of the picturesque, traditional and personal side of monarchy. Previously radicals had taken exception to the theatrical aspects of the institution: They were costly, they pandered to the irrational nature of people, and they served no useful state necessity or policy. Royal shows only encouraged the idolization of the royal family and in the process debased the worshiper.

The royal show always drew the crowds, however, and this power was hailed as a virtue in the thirties. If people demanded an outlet for their feelings, how much better was the cult of royalty than the cult of the fascist strong man. In Britain the country could revere a hero without power; it did not need to pant after a Caesar. By serving as a lightning conductor for the emotions, therefore, the Georgian monarchy was a safeguard, not a danger, for democracy.

An unsigned article in *The Political Quarterly*, a journal founded by Sidney Webb, promoted this thesis in 1937.[42] It was the conviction of many Labourites, as Kingsley Martin admitted. They believed that "If we drop the trappings of Monarchy in the gutter . . . Germany has taught us some gutter-snipe. . . may pick them up."[43] This conviction was reaffirmed in 1952 by Clement Attlee during a debate on the Civil List. It was never wise to allow government to become too dull, he announced. That was the error of the German republic after the First World War, and Hitler was allowed to get the best tunes. A "certain amount of pageantry" was desirable because it "counteracts a tendency to other forms of excitement."[44] The man in the street agreed with Attlee. In 1956 Mass-Observation discovered that 92 per cent of those polled agreed that a country with a King or Queen was less likely to go to extremes in politics.[45] Sixty-six per cent of those polled in 1966 believed that a monarchy was less likely to go to extremes than a republic. Sixty-seven per cent of those polled from the skilled working class and 56 per cent of those from unskilled working classes agreed with the statement.[46]

This more cordial approach to monarchy by Labour, however, requires further defining. Labourites who accepted the conveniences of monarchy might, by that fact, qualify as monarchists, but they were hardly traditional royalists. Most would not, with the Conservatives, refer to the "mysteries of royalty" or the "poetry of kingship." It is necessary, therefore, to distinguish between "secular" and "deferential" monarchists, although the Labour movement held both.

A secular monarchist would have agreed with Harold Nicolson: "I fear I have no mystic feeling about the Monarchy. I regard it merely as a useful institution."[47] With Beatrice Webb, he regarded the British monarchy as "an anachronism but . . . a useful anachronism, an institution for which it would be precious difficult to find an equally good substitute."[48] But he never relaxed his suspicions of royal influence and he was not reconciled to the monarchy as the symbolic head of the traditional framework of British society. The social environment of monarchy is wholly bad, Beatrice Webb wrote in 1929, and "the less the Labour Party accepts this environment the more wholesome will be its internal life."[49] The secularist, therefore, prided himself on his skeptical outlook, admitting only reluctantly (with George Bernard Shaw) that the "snobbery that surrounds the monarchy is the price we pay for its political convenience."[50] He favored reforms which would adapt the monarchy to an increasingly democratic country: Court officials should represent a wider social range; the method of conferring honors should be revised and those traditionally associated with class and privilege should fall into disuse; an extravagant royal style and expense should be avoided.[51]

On a scale of attitudes ranging from secular to deferential, most Labour leaders fell into the former category. Only a few, such as Herbert Morrison, a prominent Labour leader and Cabinet member in Labour Governments, have displayed embarrassingly strong monarchial sentiments. Harold Nicolson witnessed a display of Morrison's feelings on November 20, 1940, when Morrison was Home Secretary in Churchill's War Government:

> What amused me was Morrison's almost sobbing reference to the King's visit [to Coventry]. He spoke about the King as Goebbels might have spoken with Hitler. I admit the King does his job well. But why should Morrison speak as if he were a phenomenon?[52]

It is not possible to give statistical evidence of popular views on monarchy, either for the party, for the trade unions, or for the general working community during the reign of George V. In 1966, when the Georgian pattern was still in motion, Mass-Observation did supply some useful statistics. Of those polled from the skilled working class 50 per cent were entirely favorable to royalty, and 10 per cent largely favorable, while 11 per cent were entirely unfavorable and 4 per cent were largely unfavorable. The response from unskilled laborers was similar: 60 per cent entirely favorable and 6 per cent largely favorable with 13 per cent entirely unfavorable and 2 per cent largely unfavorable. Labour party members were less inclined toward royalty. Fifty per cent gave an entirely favorable rating, 9 per cent largely favorable, but 16 per cent were entirely unfavorable and 5 per cent were largely unfavorable.[53]

J. G. Weightman, writing "Loyal Thoughts Of An Ex-Republican" in 1953, theorized that between the wars the coolest reception to monarchy was accorded by those Labour circles in the north of England which supplied teachers, town and country councillors and Members of Parliament. At party meetings they sang "The People's Flag Is Deepest Red" instead of "God Save the King," which was considered a Conservative anthem. The throne was regarded as a Conservative preserve and the Union Jack belonged to the Conservatives because they, rather than the Labour Party, displayed it conspicuously at their sessions. This outlook was probably "already a little behind the time," admitted Weightman, and aggressive feelings against the monarchy gradually faded, although royalist feelings in 1953 were still "a rather uncomfortable, not quite respectable, emotion in many parts of the population."[54]

Most of the more educated members of the working class and lower middle class, if they approved of monarchy, were secular monarchists. Actively engaged in defining the Socialist Commonwealth, and emotionally committed to the doctrine of social equality, they granted monarchy only a sober approval based on its political convenience.

But what of the bulk of the working-class population? What is their attitude to the monarch? Richard Hoggart has made a number of revealing observations on the subject, all of which confirm the thesis of Bagehot and the peculiar strength of the psychological monarchy.[55] As an institution, he says, it is scarcely thought of by the working class; they are not royalists by principle. If interest is shown it is in the personal, for working-class people

are "personalists" and dramatists. Menfolk are observed to be either unin-
terested in royalty or vaguely hostile because it brings to mind the special
parades and spit and polish of their service days. Women are rather cynical
of the burdens borne by royal personages. They do not believe stories of
the princess who personally darns her husband's socks and tends to the
baby. Is not royalty waited on hand and foot?

At the same time, claims Hoggart, working-class people will often separate the royal family from its advisers and the government:

> It is this ability, to think of the members of the Royal Family as indi-
> viduals, caught up in a big machine manipulated by 'Them', having
> 'a real family life' only with difficulty, which allows a great many
> women in the working-classes to feel well-disposed towards Royalty
> today, and to be as interested in their more 'homely' activities as are
> women of other classes. 'It's a rotten job,' people will say, 'they get
> pushed around as much as we do.' They then feel a lot of sympathy
> for all that is expected of the monarch, feel that she and her husband
> deserve all the good-will they can get; 'She's a nice lass,' they will
> add. Other members of the Royal Family have their places, like fig-
> ures in an interesting novelett—'They say she's a mean thing';
> 'They say 'e led 'er a dog's life'; 'She likes 'er bit of fun, she does.'

They are interested, therefore, in the personal life, especially the home
life, of the royal family, and they devour every available scrap of news on
their "warm and homely ways."[56]

The progressive political forces in the country also approved of George
V's political behavior. He was considered a model constitutional monarch
because of the "sagacity and faithfulness" with which he observed the spirit of the constitution when the letter proved no complete guide.[57] The
King's resolve in this direction is noticed as early as 1894, when, as Duke
of York, he made a précis of Bagehot in which he outlined the "dignified"
and "business" functions of the Crown and appeared reconciled to be
implications of the distinction: To enhance the dignified, the Crown must
relinquish the business.

The continued exercise of business duties might involve the monarchy
in controversy and strain the effectiveness of the dignified. Or, in the
argument of Ernest Jones, the monarch could not be at once an idealized
and lovable father and a strong and domineering ruler.

The two aspects of constitutional monarchy, however, could not be
neatly divided. For the most part the Prime Minister assumed the business
functions of the executive and exercised them in the name of the Crown,
but a few business duties were still the personal responsibility of the King
and George V was called upon either to exercise them, or to consider
their use.

The monarch still had to appoint the Prime Minister and on occasion, as
in 1923 and 1931, this became more than a formality. In 1911, too, the
Crown was asked to exercise its personal prerogative of creating peers in

order to compel the Lords to accept a decision of the House of Commons. The threat of mass creations was sufficient, much to the relief of the King. Other reserve powers of the Crown—dismissing the Government, withholding assent from legislation, and dissolving Parliament without responsible advice—became subjects of serious debate during the reign of George V.

The monarchy might also influence political decisions, and the Duke of York made note of this as well in 1894:

> The Crown possesses *first* the right to be consulted, *second* the right to encourage & *third* the right to warn. And these rights may lead to a very important influence on the course of politics, especially as under a system of party government, the Monarch alone possesses a *continuous political experience.*[58]

The King insisted on these rights, especially late in his reign, and gave private advice frequently and confidently.

George V was able to perform the two functions of monarchy harmoniously for the most part: Business obligations were exercised on occasion without impairing the effectiveness of the dignified element of the Crown. (Only once, in 1931, did the use of court influence arouse the suspicions of the politicians and threaten to involve the King in political controversy.) Two virtues of George V helped make such harmony possible:

First, the King's devotion to the dignified element of monarchy enabled him to perform the business chores without arousing suspicion. His honest good will was so patent, and so widely known, that no one could believe that he was a member of one of the "contending factions" when he was on the field of politics. The bluff and honest old sailor was only doing his duty as the impartial father of the country.

Second, in the exercise of the three Bagehotian rights the King was much more evenhanded than Victoria. He had Tory prejudices and he spoke his mind in the royal closet, but unlike Victoria he did not encourage the Conservatives and reserve his warnings for the reforming parties. Nor did the King turn the right of consultation into the privilege of harassment, as his grandmother had done with Gladstone. When the King did use his influence, therefore, the politicians trusted him to run straight.

The King, however, did have his personal preferences in politics. He was comfortable with Herbert Asquith, Stanley Baldwin and J. Ramsay MacDonald as his Prime Ministers, moderate men who tried to reduce class conflict and lower political temperatures. He was less happy with Lloyd George. During the Great War the King came to appreciate the keenness and energy of the Welshman but those qualities were viewed as especially alarming in the political controversies before 1914. According to the Duke of Windsor:

> My father never really liked Lloyd George. The events of those years, and especially his oratorical blitz on the upper classes, bit too

keenly into him. He saw L. G. as a dangerous radical, pressing forward for reform at a pace that might jeopardize the whole body politic.[59]

Lloyd George's manner was partially responsible for the suspicion with which he was viewed by the Palace. He did not treat the King's staff with respect, and his secretaries, noticing this, did not even get up from their chairs when the King's private secretary came into the room. These slights were bitterly resented.[60]

George V also shared with his father a "temperamental horror of public wrangles"; he preferred "National" Governments or coalitions and the use of inter-party conferences where party leaders might reach private understandings on fundamental issues. When political passions were high George V instinctively argued for accommodation. As he asked Asquith in 1913: "Would it not be better to settle measures involving great changes in the Constitution, such as Home Rule all round, Reform of the House of Lords etc., not on Party lines, but by agreement?"[61]

In seeking the "national" approach, however, the King was not tempted to press a royal program at the expense of the parties and politicians. He had no inclination to become, as had George III, a "Patriot King." Such a role was sometimes urged upon him. The King should become like his contemporary, Alfonso XIII of Spain, the country's real source of political power, once again preside at cabinet meetings and develop a policy of his own.[62] But George V ignored such advice. Whereas Alfonso seized the opportunity to act independently of his advisers, his English counterpart made no attempt to kick against the democratic pricks. This did not leave the monarch an "inoperative ornament" of the constitution, as the ardent royalists feared. On a few occasions during his reign George V made effective use of the personal prerogative and influence in politics.

THE CONSTITUTIONAL CRISIS, 1909—1911

In the first constitutional test of his reign, the struggle over the Parliament Act, George V established a pattern of behavior that was followed faithfully by his successors. The King suppressed his subjective notions and reluctantly consented to the advice of his official advisers of the moment. Only by acting in the last resort upon the advice of his Ministers could the sovereign remove himself "from the storms and vicissitudes of party politics."

The crucial test came in November 1910, over the Government's request for "contingent guarantees" from the Crown on the matter of new creations for the Lords.[63] After the Lords had rejected the "People's Budget" in 1909 the Liberals had appealed to the country on the combined issues of the budget and the powers of House of Lords. Retaining office, the Liberals had framed a Parliament Bill which severely amputated the powers of the Upper Chamber. The measure still needed the consent of the Lords, however, and they dug in for a direct confrontation with the Commons. The escape valve in such a deadlock was the use of the royal prerogative to create peers: The King could create a Government majority in the Lords, perhaps creating as many as 500 peers.

The attitude of the Court was critical. Before his death Edward VII had informed Asquith that he could not consent to wholesale creations—or the threat of them—until after a second election on the issue of the Parliament Bill. This was a position of doubtful constitutional propriety but Asquith gave way. In advance of that second election, however, the Cabinet sought from the new monarch a secret pledge that, in the King's words, "in the event of the Government being returned with a majority at the General Election, I should use my prerogative to make peers if asked for."[64]

This request for advance guarantees was unprecedented. As Arthur Balfour, the Conservative Leader, later wrote: "A sovereign may be asked *to act*; it is no part of his duty *to promise*."[65] The request was never made of a monarch again. No Prime Minister after Asquith would have thought of asking his monarch for advance pledges; he simply assumed the monarch would comply with ministerial advice. In 1910, however, the politicians still believed that the King had the power to dismiss ministers or force a dissolution. And Asquith could envision George V refusing to create peers, at which point he could have had to withdraw his advice or resign.

The King resented the request for advance guarantees, and at first refused to comply with Asquith's advice. Had he not reconsidered, his only recourse would have been to find another administration; in 1910 this meant a Conservative Government under Balfour. Was this feasible? Later Balfour indicated that had he known guarantees was the issue, he would have been eager to form an administration. He could then have appealed to the country on the issues of Home Rule and Liberal tactics: "Does the country think it right that the King should be driven to promise, many months before the event, that the prerogative should be used, not to get the Parliament Bill through but to get the Parliament Bill through *in the exact form desired by Mr. Redmond*?"[66] By choosing the most favorable grounds on which to wage an election, the Conservatives might have won a majority.

Balfour was not given the opportunity. He was outmaneuvered by Asquith, aided by Lord Knollys, private secretary to the King, and a friend of the Liberal Ministers. First, the King was bullied. If he refused to give guarantees the Cabinet would immediately resign and at the next election raise the cry, "The King and the Peers against the People." Moreover, Asquith declined to allow the monarch to consult with Balfour and Lord Lansdowne, the Conservative Leader in the House of Lords. It was Lord Knollys, however, who exercised the decisive influence. He argued that the Government's request was constitutionally correct; and he insisted that the King had no other alternative because Balfour would decline to form an administration. In the face of such pressure, the King relented and agreed to give secret guarantees, although "I dislike having to do this very much."[67]

In obtaining the pledge from George V Asquith was not, as his biographer admits, "over-delicate." He exerted great pressure, and seemed determined to keep the King in the dark about the attitude of Balfour. Clearly he feared that the King might refuse his advice if he knew an alternative administration was available. Asquith's refusal to permit the King to see the opposition leaders raised a serious constitutional question: Did the duty of the King to take advice from his Ministers mean he must be forbidden the knowledge that he had another set of ministers available? Was the King to act as a conscript of the party in power?

Lord Knollys, however, has drawn the sharpest criticism for his role in the crisis. Although the King's private secretary, he apparently deliberately concealed important information from his master. Seven days before the death of Edward VII Knollys attended a meeting at Lambeth Palace between the Archbishop of Canterbury, Balfour and Lord Esher. At this session Balfour made it clear that he would form a government "to prevent the King being put in the position contemplated by the demand for the creation of Peers."[68] In November 1910, however, Knollys withheld this information from George V and assured him that Balfour would decline to form an administration. Because he suppressed vital information Knollys has been roundly condemned. He played a "dubious part" and a "devious role" in the crisis, says Kenneth Young, one of Balfour's biographers.[69]

But while his methods were dubious, Knollys' advice was undoubtedly politically sound. Had the Crown changed the Government it would have acted as a partisan, and raised the issue of royal favoritism. By following the advice of Knollys, the Crown, unlike the Lords, avoided a direct, public confrontation with the Liberals. Thus, as Roy Jenkins has convincingly argued, "the nation and institution of constitutional monarchy owe Knollys a deep debt of gratitude." The consequences of rejecting a Liberal Government "in the explosive atmosphere of pre-1914 England, might have been far-reaching."[70]

Politicians of the Left subjected the royal actions to a close scrutiny because the struggle over the Parliament Bill was not an academic debate: It was a vital contest for the political power necessary to determine the fate of progressive legislation. Their confidence in monarchy flowed from the decision of George V to abide strictly by the doctrine of ministerial responsibility. From the influence of Knollys in 1910, therefore, grew the harmonious relations the Crown enjoyed with the Labour Party in the 1920s and 1930s.

Conservatives of course felt no gratitude for the part monarchy played in the passage of the Parliament Bill, and a few hotheads even talked of a censure motion directed against the King. George V had allowed himself to become a pawn of the Liberal Government and Party, they claimed, and had permitted the royal prerogative to be used on behalf of revolutionary measures proposed by a temporary majority. This Conservative fury was the product of bitter disappointment: Because George V had known Tory prejudices, Conservatives regarded him as a political ally. Perhaps, as Roger Fulford speculates, the Lords even "hardened their hearts" in the belief they could rely on Palace support.[71] Such expectations probably rested on the memory of Victoria's partisan activities, a part of the unhappy political legacy of the Queen. Unlike his grandmother, however, George V did not seek to undermine Liberal legislation or to place the Crown at the service of Conservative politicians.

Still, it was incorrect to assume, as some Conservatives did, that the caution of George V would lead to an automatic and mechanical exercise of the royal prerogative by his Ministers. As subsequent episodes suggest, George V was not a mere conscript of the government of the day.

HOME RULE CRISIS, 1912–1914

Until shorn of its veto the House of Lords served as a dependable second line of defense for the Conservatives against undesirable legislation. Usually passive under Conservative Governments, the Lords became active under the Liberals, and, as Lord Rosebery complained in 1894, their activity was "entirely exercised in opposition to the Government."[72] In 1911, however, that barrier to progressive legislation was broken. And in 1912 Asquith offered a Home Rule Bill for Ireland, promising to fulfill a policy Gladstone had first adopted for the Party in 1886. Ireland, including the predominantly Protestant counties of Ulster, would obtain a measure of autonomy from Britain.

Irish Home Rule, however, provoked a bitter struggle between the two parties which soon threatened to involve the Crown. The Conservative opposition even entertained the possibility of civil war as a means of avoiding the "disruption" of the United Kingdom and the "coercion" of Ulster into an Irish Parliament. Their fury was increased by their legislative impotence: Because of the Parliament Bill the Liberals could force Home Rule through Parliament by the summer of 1914. The Lords could no longer force a general election, at which Conservatives were certain English public opinion would rise "in a gust of passion"[73] and end Liberal rule.

Conservatives decided to fall back upon the Crown as another line of defense. George V must be persuaded to exercise latent royal prerogatives and (1) refuse assent to the Home Rule Bill, thereby forcing the Government to resign; or (2) dismiss his Liberal Ministers and place confidence in those who would retain the unity of the realm or (3) dissolve Parliament and ensure a general election. Bonar Law, the Conservative leader, bluntly told the King in May 1912:

> Our desire has been to keep the Crown out of our struggles, but the Government have brought it in. Your only chance is that they should resign within two years. If they don't you must either accept the Home Rule Bill, or dismiss your Ministers and choose others who will support you in vetoing it: and in either case, half your subjects will think you have acted against them.[74]

The Conservative tactic raised serious questions, all freely aired in the public press between 1912 and 1914. What was the extent of the Crown's powers in these matters? Was the right to refuse assent, unexercised since

Queen Anne, not dead through disuse? Could the King still dismiss a Government and dissolve Parliament on his own initiative? More importantly, was it wise to break established conventions even if the legal right remained? Would not political difficulties follow?

Rival political camps pressed their advice upon the Court. According to Bonar Law, the prerogative of veto was not dead because the Liberals had destroyed the veto of the Lords, the legal buffer between Crown and Commons. He and Lord Lansdowne, Leader of the House of Lords, also urged dismissal of Asquith as the only means of averting civil war.[75] Arthur Balfour predicted Home Rule would shake the Empire and shatter the discipline of the army. To avoid such disasters the King had a duty to change his advisers.[76] Lord Esher, a private adviser, urged appointment of a "neutral statesman" as Prime Minister until the electorate pronounced on Home Rule.[77]

In the Liberal camp Asquith produced his memorandum* on the proper role of the monarch. He rejected the idea that the King could withhold assent, pointing out that the veto had not been exercised for 200 years. The principle that the King must, in the last resort, act upon the advice of his Ministers was firmly established. The right to dismiss ministers still applied, he admitted, but had not been used since 1834. Should the King dismiss ministers holding the confidence of Commons he would render the Crown "the football of contending factions." To dismiss the Government would entail consequences "very injurious to the authority of the Crown."

Asquith's counsel prevailed at court, although the Prime Minister thought the King was sometimes a little wobbly, and Conservative tactics were rejected. That decision was communicated to the Opposition late in 1913. George V could still exercise influence, however, and this was unmistakably applied on behalf of the Conservative case. The King tried to persuade Asquith to seek a public mandate on Home Rule, or, failing this, to exclude Ulster from the Home Rule arrangements. "No doubt," says Roy Jenkins, the King wanted "Whig men and Tory measures."[78]

George V also encouraged a compromise agreement, to be reached at private sessions attended by captains of the opposing political armies. Largely to appease the King, Asquith and Law held several secret sessions in late 1913 and early 1914, although both leaders were skeptical of their value. In fact, no agreement emerged and Law, misunderstanding a remark of Asquith, was convinced thereafter that the Prime Minister was not a man of his word.[79]

When the Government was ready to consider excluding Ulster the King repeatedly pressed for a non-party conference, which was finally convened at Buckingham Palace in July 1914. Differences were too wide, however, and the conference broke down. The King was left to console himself with the possibility of "a more friendly understanding."[80]

---

*See Appendix B.

George V therefore deliberately chose to restrict the business role of monarchy during the Home Rule crisis, following a pattern established in 1910. His influence was used on behalf of compromise, but the non-party conference, a favorite device, failed. There was some question as to whether or not the monarch should even encourage such conferences. Inevitably the practice interfered with the normal working of party politics and Parliamentary Government, and threatened to draw the Crown into politics. Conservatives praised the King for using his powers to advise and to warn, expecting the royal influence to weaken the will of the Government, but many Liberals regarded non-party conferences as attempts to circumvent the Parliament Bill. In these circumstances the Crown risked the possibility of open criticism, and the charge of political partisanship.

WAR AND "THE KING'S MEN"

The Great War sharpened the division of labor between the monarch and the Prime Minister, with the latter virtually monopolizing business duties. The character of Lloyd George, who became First Minister in December 1916, aided the process. George V was disturbed to discover that even his Bagehotian rights received short shrift: He was more often "informed" than "consulted." Such unorthodox methods, against which the King protested in vain, were the trademark of the little Welshman, "the nearest thing England has known to a Napoleon, a supreme ruler maintaining himself by individual achievement."[81] Eventually the King warmed to Lloyd George and expressed regret at his downfall in 1922 but during the war he withheld his full confidence. After an interview with George V in October 1917, Colonel House recorded in his diary:

> He (the King) touched, with a tinge of bitterness, upon the assumption of autocratic powers by some of his Prime Ministers. He plainly referred to Lloyd George, and I could see there was considerable feeling lurking under the surface.[82]

Differences between monarch and Prime Minister soon extended to wartime strategy and military leadership, areas where the King, as Head of the Services, could wield considerable influence.

The monarch by tradition took an interest in the Services and voiced opinion on the higher promotions; George V kept up a close personal association with ranking admirals and generals during the war. This royal interest was not passive, as George V first revealed in 1915. Failures in Allied strategy had convinced him—and others—by the summer of 1915 that Sir John French, a mercurial cavalry officer, was unfit to continue as Commander-in-Chief of the British Forces in France. Doubts were reinforced by criticism of French conveyed privately to the King by Sir Douglas Haig, Commander of the British First Army, and an old and much favored friend of the royal family. Haig urged dismissal of his superior, suggesting it take place after a battlefield reversal. Using his private knowledge George V pressed the Government for a change in command, while he encouraged Haig to submit secret reports to him on affairs in Flanders, though confessing "If anyone acted like that, and told tales out of school, he would at school be called a sneak."[83] The general, who replaced French in December 1915, continued to enjoy the powerful protective shelter of the King's goodwill throughout the war, even at a time when the Prime Minister was actively canvassing his dismissal. In the first significant upheaval in wartime leadership, therefore, the King played an active role. The editor of Haig's private papers concludes that the King "was far from acting as a mere figurehead and that, almost as much as Asquith, he was responsible for the change in command."[84]

The monarch's position at the center of authority, with confidences from civil and military leaders, took on special significance when a rift over strategy developed between the politicians and the generals. The King, with a strong Service bias, threw his weight behind the "brass hats" and against the "amateur strategists," one of whom was his Prime Minister. He was in sympathy with the view that there was danger of "the fidgety desire of men [politicians] who do not know the intricate [military] machine and try and tinker with it."[85] Strategic control should rest in the hands of the trained technicians of war.

Royal support for the generals was of special importance in 1917 and early in 1918, as the contest for control of strategy intensified, because Lloyd George was uncertain of his own political security; accordingly, the royal influence was a factor of "the utmost weight" in a "critical division and distribution of loyalties."[86]

As Prime Minister, Lloyd George promoted no settled strategical plan but he was convinced the Haig-Robertson (Sir William Robertson, who, in December 1915, became Chief of the Imperial General Staff and therefore Military Adviser to the War Cabinet) strategy of smashing the German army by continuous offensives on the Western Front was a failure. Moreover, it produced heavy casualties and Lloyd George was not prepared to be "a butcher's boy driving cattle to the slaughter."[87] He was inclined to stand on the defensive in France while knocking out such props of Germany as Austria-Hungary and Turkey. In 1917 he shared the defensive outlook of Marshal Pétain: The Allies should wait until the Americans arrived.

Unwilling to run the political risks of dislodging his military advisers, Lloyd George resorted to indirect methods. He advocated "unified command," a principle he valued in itself, as a way of neutralizing his generals. The Calais Conference of February 26 and 27, 1917, was his first flanking action.[88] On February 24, the War Cabinet, without the presence of Robertson, authorized the Prime Minister to secure unity of command in France in preparation for the spring offensive of General Robert Neville, the new French commander of the North and Northeast. Armed with this directive Lloyd George summoned Haig and Robertson to Calais, ostensibly to discuss transportation problems, and confronted them with a hastily conceived plan for rearranging the command structure. The British Commander-in-Chief would fall under the direct command of Neville,

referred to by Haig as "a junior *foreign* commander." Haig immediately appealed to the King, who had not been informed of the Cabinet decision
until February 28. His response was recorded in Haig's diary for March 9:

> The King was most pleased to see me and stated that he would "sup-
> port me through thick and thin," but I must be careful not to resign,
> because Lloyd George would then appeal to the country for support
> and would probably come back with a great majority, as L. G. was at
> present very popular it seems. . . . We went over the whole Calais
> Conference. . . . He was furious with Lloyd George, and said he was
> to see him tomorrow.[89]

This was unusual advice from a constitutional monarch. But the King
and his court advisers repeatedly cautioned Haig and Robertson not to
provoke the Prime Minister too far, lest he call for an election and emerge
as a civilian dictator.

Lloyd George was forced to accept a compromise at Calais; Haig was
subordinated only for the duration of the Neville campaign, which ended
in failure. In the autumn of 1918, however, military disaster in Italy
prompted renewed demands for a unified command. In November an
Allied Supreme War Council was constituted with Britain, Italy and
France contributing a permanent Military Representative. The organization finally gave Lloyd George an opportunity to sidetrack one of his military advisers. Robertson refused appointment to the new post and
declined to work as C.I.G.S. under the new arrangements. George V still
urged his retention but Lloyd George interpreted Robertson's actions as
tantamount to military supremacy. He pressed his view upon the King's
private secretary. If the King insisted upon Robertson remaining on his
own terms the Crown would have to find other ministers. "The Government *must* govern, whereas this was practically military dictation." The
private secretary assured the Prime Minister that His Majesty "had no idea
of making such insistence."[90]

Ironically the replacement of Robertson allowed no change in strategy.
The German offensive in the spring of 1918 made it necessary to concen-
trate on the Western Front, where Haig continued as Commander-in-
Chief.

Evidence therefore suggests that George V was no mere cipher during
the war. Exercise of influence, however, raises questions of its use. Historians have generally censured the King's encouragement of a secret correspondence behind the back of the Prime Minister. Imprudent, too, was the
persistent support for generals disliked and distrusted by the Crown's civil
advisers. Lloyd George believed, or claimed to believe, that a conspiracy
was afoot in 1918 to drive him from office. In his *War Memoirs* he refers to
"a cabal which would overthrow the existing War Cabinet and especially
its Chief, and enthrone a Government which would be practically the
nominee and menial of this military party."[91] Robertson was regarded as
leader of the plot. The Crown might very easily have been caught up in
unsavory political machinations.

Support for the generals also embraced their wartime strategy. Should the King bear some responsibility for its persistent application? If so, this could only invite criticism, and criticism inevitably damages a reputation for impartiality upon which the effectiveness of the dignified role of monarchy is based. Some critics of the Western Front strategy have indicted the King. Kingsley Martin's harsh judgment is an example. Royal support for Haig, he claims, probably prolonged the war and "added greatly to the number of young Englishmen who died in it."[92]

THE APPOINTMENT OF BALDWIN

Among the monarch's personal prerogatives, and occasional duties, is the appointment of the Prime Minister. According to Ivor Jennings it is the only remaining business duty of primary importance.[93] In its fulfillment the Crown in theory is granted complete liberty of choice, but in fact most appointments are well defined and become only a formality.

There is no difficulty when a Government is successful in a general election: the Prime Minister remains in office, as was the case during the reign of George V with Asquith in 1910, Lloyd George in 1918, Bonar Law in 1922 and Ramsay MacDonald in November 1931. No doubt arises, either, when the opposition earns a majority in the House of Commons. Baldwin was immediately summoned to Buckingham Palace after the victory of his party in 1924. The party system did not work so smoothly in 1923 and 1929. In the first election the Conservatives remained the largest party in the House, but without a majority, and the Liberals and Labourites combined to bring down the Baldwin Government. The King decided to send for Ramsay MacDonald, who became the first Labour Prime Minister, on the grounds that he was the leader of the next largest party. The real decision, however, was made when the Conservatives and Liberals decided not to combine or keep Labour out of office. In 1929 Labour did not obtain a majority but it was the largest of the three parties, and so MacDonald was invited to try to form a government. Constitutional authorities have not faulted the conduct of the King on these occasions.

When the Prime Minister resigns or dies in office between general elections, however, the monarch assumes personal responsibility for appointing his successor. He is, accordingly, likely to become associated with political controversy. Even in these two eventualities, however, the monarch's freedom of action is limited in practice. Under the modern party system he must select a politician who commands wide support in his party. No Prime Minister in modern times could say, as did Charles James Fox, "I am a minister because the King made me so." A decision made by Bonar Law in 1922, after he had brought down the Coalition Government of Lloyd George, suggests the value placed upon party approval in recent times. Law refused, in his first audience with George V, to kiss hands until after a party meeting had elected him leader.[94]

In addition, the parties have adopted formal election procedures for choosing new leaders before appointment, although this undoubtedly infringes upon the royal prerogative. Election before appointment restricts the monarch's freedom of choice—he can hardly refuse a party nominee and send for another—but it also relieves him of a heavy responsibility.

But Conservatives did not adopt election procedures until 1965 and so George V faced a problem when Bonar Law resigned because of ill health in the spring of 1923. No single figure stood out as the heir apparent, as Chamberlain did in 1937 and Eden in 1955.[95] Lord Curzon and Stanley Baldwin emerged as rivals for the succession.

In theory George V could have made the selection himself, and without advice. Supposedly Victoria had made a personal choice of Lord Rosebery in 1894, not consulting Gladstone about his successor. Traditionally, however, the monarch seeks the advice of the retiring Prime Minister, whose judgment becomes decisive. In 1923, however, Bonar Law declined to advise the Crown officially on a successor, although he thought Curzon would in fact succeed him, and conveyed his expectations to Curzon and Baldwin.[96] Privately Law suggested to intimates a preference for Baldwin. George V chose to consult two elder statesmen in the party.[97] Lord Salisbury, the Lord President of the Council, pointed out the imposing claims of Curzon based on seniority and experience. Arthur Balfour, except for Bonar Law the only living Tory ex-premier, expressed the view that because of the rise of Labour the Prime Minister ought to be in the Commons. This would disqualify Curzon. Balfour's advice reinforced a conviction of the King. In 1921 Lord Robert Cecil, anticipating the collapse of the Coalition Government, had urged the monarch to consider Lord Grey as a prospective Prime Minister. In answer the King had ventured the opinion that a Prime Minister, after the Parliament Bill, should reside in the House of Commons.[98]

Baldwin, in fact, was finally summoned. Had the King, then, acted upon his own preference after receiving conflicting advice, and decided for himself? Had he preserved the reality of the personal prerogative of appointment?

Until recently the episode of 1923 was frequently cited as an example of the monarch's independent exercise of the prerogative. In 1955, however, Robert Blake's biography of Bonar Law, based on personal papers, offered a far different story.[99] According to Blake, when Law's principal private secretary, Lieutenant-Colonel Ronald Waterhouse, presented Law's letter of resignation to the King, he also presented a memorandum on the succession heavily loaded in favor of Baldwin, and stated that it "practically expressed the views" of his master. This memorandum had been written by J. C. C. Davidson, a friend of Baldwin's. Two days later Waterhouse again saw the King's private secretary and indicated Law's personal preference for Baldwin. Blake maintains that Law knew nothing of the memorandum or of Waterhouse's statements. Yet George V sent for Baldwin, believing this to be the wish of his retiring Prime Minister.

Davidson himself, however, recently divulged new information while dictating his recollection of the episode.[100] He claims his memorandum was drafted at the request of the King's private secretary, as the opinion of a well-informed member of the Conservative Party in Parliament. Waterhouse was probably shown the document only on his second visit to the

Palace, at which time he expressed the opinion that the document practically reflected the outlook of Law. Therefore no deception was intended—or practiced.

If Davidson's version is correct, and there is no reason to believe otherwise, George V tried to canvass Conservative opinion, and to choose the candidate most acceptable to the party, and to his outgoing prime minister. The appointment was derived from the party, although the King assumed the responsiblity.

CRISIS OF 1931

In 1931 the King was able to exercise his reserve powers again, this time in commissioning Ramsay MacDonald to form a National Government. Unlike the selection of Baldwin in 1923, however, this appointment was to provoke controversy.

A financial crisis in August created a political crisis and drew the King onto the political field.[101] London bankers informed the Labour Government that the country was on the edge of bankruptcy, brought on by a serious run on sterling. The cause of the trouble was diagnosed as political in nature: a lack of confidence in the British Government on the part of foreign investers. Only if the Government proposed a balanced budget, involving a sharp cutback in unemployment benefits, would foreign bankers grant sufficient credits to save the British pound.

The Cabinet was unable to agree on economics, however, and on the morning of August 23 the Prime Minister informed the King that the resignation of his Government was imminent because of internal divisions. He advised the monarch to confer with the spokesmen of the other political parties. From these discussions emerged a National Government under MacDonald.

It was natural that the King should summon the Conservative and Liberal leaders to Buckingham Palace immediately after his session with MacDonald. Only they, acting together, could form a new administration. When a Cabinet decides to resign, the monarch is also free to consult "what party leaders he pleases to determine what Government Parliamentary exigencies demand."[102] The fact that no party had a majority, however, made the final outcome difficult to forecast: It also left the King a degree of choice. The Labour Cabinet expected Baldwin to form a new government based on a Conservative-Liberal coalition. An administration of personalities or an all-party coalition were also possibilities. Apparently a coalition was even discussed by the Cabinet on August 23. "This, he [MacDonald] intimated, was what the King desired and might propose," Beatrice Webb recorded in her diary.[103]

The "crisis" psychology apparently affected the King at the time. He shared the common belief that the country was facing bankruptcy. (In the judgment of the Queen, it was "quite the worst one [crisis] for our poor unfortunate country" since the Great War.[104]) He was convinced therefore that he must name a new government immediately, hopefully one that could not only obtain a majority in Commons but also enlist widespread popular support.

The King's thinking was shaped by Sir Herbert Samuel, the acting Liberal leader, who happened to arrive at Buckingham Palace before Baldwin on the afternoon of August 23. Samuel argued that the best solution was for MacDonald to remain in office with a purely Labour Cabinet. Painful economics would be more palatable to the working class if perfomed by a Labour Government. If Labour resigned, the best alternative would be a national administration headed by MacDonald and composed of representatives from all three parties. A solely Conservative or a Conservative-Liberal combination would be the least effective way of meeting the emergency.[105] When Baldwin arrived he acquiesced in Samuel's advice, at least to the point of agreeing to cooperate.

George V was receptive to Samuel's suggested alternative to a purely Labour Government. As Sidney Webb observed in September 1931, English monarchs "always have a hankering" for administrations that sink party interests in a common purpose.[106] George V was a favored monarch in this respect: Nearly half of his reign was under "National" or coalition governments. The King's appeal to MacDonald on August 23 was apparently decisive in persuading him to remain. The following day, after a conference with the other party leaders, he resigned as Premier of a Labour Cabinet, only to emerge as Premier of a National Government composed of personalities.

The collapse of the second Labour Government and its replacement by a National administration transformed the political scene. Labour chose to go into active opposition, and even expelled MacDonald from its ranks. In October the party lost over 200 seats (288 to 52) in the general election, and was not to form another government until 1945. The National Government, composed mostly of Conservatives, won overwhelming public endorsement and held power throughout the 1930s.

For the King the 1931 crisis was the supreme political moment of his life. It highlighted the business role of monarchy, and demonstrated beyond doubt that the King was much more than a symbol of national solidarity. The monarch's own advisers thought he had been able "to play the Sovereign for once, and give a lead to his rattled Ministers."[107] In fulfilling his business obligation, however, the King drew attention to himself, thereby running the risk of becoming involved in controversy. And questions about the monarch's role in the transactions of 1931 were immediately raised. Had George V exceeded his constitutional authority? Had he, as Herbert Morrison charged, "drawn the monarchy into politics, and pretty dangerous politics at that."[108]

Criticism of the King's actions on constitutional grounds focused on two points:[109] First, that MacDonald was the King's personal nominee; he had become Prime Minister solely at the instance of the Crown. When the personal records of the chief actors of 1931 were published, however, they destroyed the argument that the King had imposed his will on the politicians. Samuel indicated that George V had invited MacDonald to form a National Government on advice "unanimously tendered to him" by party leaders.[110] These accounts confirmed the importance of the King's role: He drew the politicians together, solicited their advice, and appealed to

MacDonald to remain in office. But they all agreed that the monarch had acted with due constitutional propriety.

Critics also contended that the King should appoint a person as Prime Minister only if he possessed the approval and support of his own party. MacDonald did not have the confidence of his party, and was soon separated from it. This argument, however, has not appealed to historians and constitutional authorities. They point out that if adopted the principle would severely limit the monarch's freedom to select, after receiving the best advice he could obtain, the person who in his judgment was best suited to form a government and find majority support for it in the House of Commons. It would also make the statesman "the prisoner of his party organization" and tend to raise party interest above the national welfare.[111]

George V was also indicted by a few critics for the "political" mistake of appointing MacDonald.[112] Labour received a grave injury in 1931, it is argued, and this might have aroused the Party's resentment and undermined the position and strength of the monarchy. Most Labourites, however, did not charge the King with willful partisanship and the monarch's reputation for neutrality was also safeguarded by the Crown's caution after the formation of the National Government. George V voiced no personal political preference and the Government received no open endorsement. This contrasted with the established practice of the Belgian monarchy for giving public support for policies and governments on supreme occasions.[113] In 1926, for example, King Albert commended to the country a government which had just been created to solve a financial crisis. George V never bestowed the royal blessing on a government or policy.[114] He tried to be scrupulously impartial, and to give the appearance of it, which minimized the danger which fulfillment of business obligations held for the dignified image of monarchy.

Considering his right-wing prejudices and "private war with the twentieth century" it was fortunate for the country and the monarchy that George V had a limited political role, and suppressed his personal feelings when fulfilling his constitutional duties. Only a studied neutrality enabled him to accept "with acquiescence—if not always with uncomplaining acquiescence—the larger transformations" of his twenty-five years on the throne.[115] Yet the outlook that disqualified him as a modern political leader enhanced the King's dignified image. Late in his reign he became a beloved grandfather figure because he did not keep pace with his age; his settled habits and Victorian appearance made him, according to an observer in 1935, "A centre of calm in a blowing wind of change—a signal of comfort and assurance on a ship driving rapidly forward."[116] Queen Mary's unchanging style of dress—the toque, the coiffure, the parasol—also reinforced this image of the Georgian monarchy.[117]

The great popularity of the Georgian fashion was not fully realized until the Silver Jubilee of the King and Queen in 1935. Even the royal couple was surprised at the mass public demonstration of affection and loyalty, which included even the poorer sections of London. The King's death on January 20, 1936 also stirred popular emotions and brought an outpouring of public grief. But it was the following reign, "the strange interlude of

Edward VIII," which most clearly demonstrated the depth of the Georgian synthesis.

[1] Harold Nicolson, *King George V*, p. 106.
[2] Sebastian Haffner, "The Renascence of Monarchy," *The Twentieth Century*, June 1953, p. 415.
[3] This list does not include those small sovereign principalities of Monaco (0.6 square miles) and Liechtenstein (62 square miles).
[4] The phrase of Edward Shils and Michael Young, "The Meaning of the Coronation," *Sociological Review*, II, July 1955, p. 76.
[5] Sebastian Haffner, *op. cit.*, p. 415.
[6] Thomas Babington Macaulay, *The History of England from the Accession of James II*, II, 519–20.
[7] Reginald Viscount Esher, *Journals and Letters*, IV, 147.
[8] Harold Nicolson, *King George V*, p. 326.
[9] Lord David Cecil, "The Reigning Royalty of Europe," *Life Magazine*, August 5, 1957, p. 61.
[10] House of Commons *Parliamentary Debates* (July 9, 1952), Fifth Series, Volume 503, 1365.
[11] Ernest Jones, *Essays in Applied Psychoanalysis*, I, 229.
[12] David and Anthony Jay, *The English*, p. 184.
[13] Edward Shils and Michael Young, *op. cit.*, p. 78.
[14] Samuel H. Beer and Adam Ulam, eds., *Patterns of Government: The Major Political Systems of Europe*, p. 71.
[15] Eric A. Nordlinger, *The Working-Class Tories: Authority, Deference and Stable Democracy*, p. 242.
[16] Winston S. Churchill, *Great Contemporaries*, p. 280.
[17] The appraisal of G.K. Chesterton, writing in *The Illustrated London News*, January 25, 1936.
[18] James Pope-Hennessy, *Queen Mary*, p. 359. Max Beerbohm expressed the view of many clever people in a famous playlet of his on the royal couple, which turned on the double refrain: "The King is duller than the Queen" and "The Queen is duller than the King." (See S.N. Behrman, *Portrait of Max*, pp. 100–01.)
[19] See Michael Stewart's article "Labour and the Monarchy" in *Fabian Journal*, October 1952.
[20] All statistics are taken from David Butler and Jennie Freeman, *British Political Facts, 1900–1967*, Second Edition, pp. 107 and 219 '.
[21] Raymond Postage, *The Life of George Lansbury*, p. 225.
[22] The testimony of J.R. Clynes, one of the new Cabinet Members. Harold Nicolson, *King George V*, p. 387.
[23] See Harold Nicolson, *King George V*, pp. 391–92, on this episode.
[24] James Robert Rhodes, ed., *Memoirs Of A Conservative*, pp. 177–78.
[25] These activities are described by John W. Wheeler-Bennett in his *King George VI*, pp. 157–72.
[26] *Ibid.*, p. 157.
[27] J. H. Thomas, *When Labour Rules*, p. 47.
[28] *Labour Party, 23rd Annual Report* (June 26–29), pp. 250–51. The full resolution read: "That the Royal Family is no longer necessary as part of the British Constitution, and the Labour Party is therefore asked to state definitely its view of this matter." A second resolution was also offered: "That the hereditary principle in the British Constitution be abolished." The chairman ruled that it was covered by the first and the resolution was not even debated.
[29] House of Commons *Parliamentary Debates* (May 24, 1937), Fifth Series, Volume 324, 40.
[30] Kingsley Martin, *The Crown and the Establishment*, pp. 54–55.
[31] Leonard Woolf promoted this argument in *Quack, Quack!*, especially pp. 32–34. A Canadian psychologist, Percy Black, has given a full consideration of this theme in *The Mystique of Modern Monarchy*.
[32] As early as 1911 Ramsay MacDonald has tempered his remarks on monarchy. He wrote in *The Socialist Movement*, pp. 150–51: "The virtues of republicanism and the conveniences of a monarchy are subjects of abstract interest which may ruffle for an hour the surface of debating societies, but in this country and under present circumstances, they do not make a ripple in Parliamentary controversy or take up a line in Parliamentary

programmes . . . from the purely practical point of view [as long as there was democratic control of government], Socialism . . . does not consider republicanism of essential importance."

[33] Ivan Maisky, *Journey into the Past*, p. 182.

[34] Henry Pelling, *A Short History of the Labour Party*, p. 44.

[35] Quoted in Samuel H. Beer, *Modern British Politics*, p. 142.

[36] *Ibid.*, p. 135.

[37] Ivan Maisky, *Journey into the Past*, p. 216.

[38] *Ibid.*, p. 182.

[39] *Ibid.*, p. 178.

[40] Michael Stewart, "Labour and the Monarchy," *Fabian Journal*, October 1952, p. 18. The paragraph above is based on his article.

[41] Argued by Laski in *Parliamentary Government in England*.

[42] A Historian, "The King, the Cabinet, and the People," *The Political Quarterly*, VIII, 1937, pp. 1–6.

[43] Kingsley Martin, "The Evolution Of Popular Monarchy," *The Political Quarterly*, VII, 1936, pp. 155–56.

[44] House of Commons *Parliamentary Debates* (July 9, 1952), Fifth Series, Volume 5-3, 1328.

[45] Tom Harrison, et. al., *Britain Revisited*, p. 231.

[46] Leonard M. Harris, *Long To Reign Over Us?*, p. 150.

[47] Harold Nicolson's comment appearing in his diary for January 17, 1950, while he was preparing the official biography of George V. See *Diaries And Letters*, III, 184.

[48] Margaret Cole, ed., *Beatrice Webb's Diaries, 1924–1932*, p. 200.

[49] *Ibid.*

[50] Cited in Michael Stewart, "Labour and the Monarchy," *Fabian Journal*, October 1952, p. 17.

[51] Michael Stewart has made a summary of these desired reforms in his article, "Labour and the Monarchy."

[52] Harold Nicolson, *Diaries And Letters*, II, 128.

[53] Leonard M. Harris, *Long To Reign Over Us?*, pp. 144–45.

[54] J. G. Weightman, "Loyal Thoughts Of An Ex-Republican," *The Twentieth Century*, June 1953, pp. 406–07.

[55] Richard Hoggart, *The Uses of Literacy*, pp. 92–93.

[56] It is said that the Trade Union newspaper in the thirties, the *Daily Herald*, spent more time on royal activities than its competitors. So Harold Laski claimed in *Parliamentary Government in England*, p. 331.

[57] See Winston S. Churchill's tribute in *Great Contemporaries*, p. 282. On this theme see E. T. Williams, "The Crown and the Prime Minister," *The Listener*, January 1, 1953. The following discussion is indebted to his brief but excellent analysis.

[58] Harold Nicolson, *King George V*, p. 62.

[59] Duke of Windsor, "Reflections Of a One-Time Prince Of Wales," *McCall's*, June 1969, p. 107.

[60] See Robert Rhodes James, ed., *Memoirs of a Conservative*, p. 67.

[61] Harold Nicolson, *King George V.*, p. 224.

[62] This bold course was urged by Hugh Cecil, *Conservatism*, pp. 223–33 and Sir Charles Petrie, *Monarchy*, especially pp. 271–301. On page 300 Petrie expresses the hope that "Under the cover of the monarchy did political democracy gain its first, and under cover of the monarchy it must lose its last, hold upon the Constitution."

[63] Roy Jenkins, *Mr. Balfour's Poodle* is a very lively account of this episode. See also his *Asquith*, pp. 218–22. Harold Nicolson, *King George V*, pp. 125–39, records the outlook of the Palace on guarantees, and Kenneth Young, *Arthur James Balfour*, pp. 300–09, gives the viewpoint of Balfour and the Conservatives.

[64] Harold Nicolson, *King George V*, p. 138.

[65] Quoted in Kenneth Young, *Arthur James Balfour*, p. 305.

[66] *Ibid.*, p. 301. John Redmond was the leader of the Irish Parliamentary Party.

[67] The pledge was extracted from the King on November 16 during a meeting between the King, Asquith, and Lord Crewe, the Liberal leader in the Lords. See Lord Derby's memorandum in Randolph S. Churchill, *Lord Derby: "King of Lancashire,"* pp. 126–27, on this session.

[68] Quoted in Harold Nicolson, *King George V*, pp. 129–30. Nicolson claims Edward VII was informed of Balfour's willingness to form a government a week before his death. Jenkins, *Mr. Balfour's Poodle*, pp. 177–78, suggests the King was given the news the day before he died. Kenneth Young, *Arthur James Balfour*, p. 293, believes Balfour's offer was never brought to the attention of Edward. The point does not seem important. The Lambeth Palace meeting was held on April 29, 1910, and Edward died May 6.

[69] Kenneth Young, *Arthur James Balfour*, p. 302. See also Sir Charles Petrie, *The Modern British Monarchy*, pp. 107–08. Young and Petrie are convinced that the dangerous events of 1910–1911 would have been avoided if Balfour had been able to form an administration. Had the Conservatives been beaten at the polls, Petrie speculates, the House of Lords "might have accepted the verdict, and the threat to swamp that body by the creation of new peers would not have been necessary." Therefore "Knollys has a great deal for which to answer at the bar of British history." But these two authors do not consider the probable response of the Left at the time. For the King to have rejected the Liberal government, as Roy Jenkins has argued (*Asquith*, p. 220), "might well have affected not only his personal position but the whole future of the British monarchy."

[70] Roy Jenkins, *Mr. Balfour's Poodle*, p. 183.

[71] Simon Nowell-Smith, ed., *Edwardian England 1901–1914*, p. 30.

[72] Quoted in Roy Jenkins, *Mr. Balfour's Poodle*, p. 34.

[73] The phrase and fervent hope of L. S. Amery, *My Political Life*, I, 406. See also Robert Blake, *The Unknown Prime Minister*, p. 131.

[74] Harold Nicolson, *King George V*, p. 200.

[75] Robert Blake, *The Unknown Prime Minister*, p. 152.

[76] Blanche Dugdale, *Arthur James Balfour*, II, 68.

[77] Reginald Viscount Esher, *Journals and Letters*, I, pp. 147–48.

[78] Roy Jenkins, *Asquith*, p. 296.

[79] Harold Nicolson, *King George V*, p. 232.

[80] *Ibid.*, p. 243.

[81] A.J.P. Taylor, *English History 1914–1945*, p. 73.

[82] Quoted in Lord Beaverbrook, *Men And Power, 1917–1918*, pp. 204–05.

[83] Robert Blake, ed., *The Private Papers of Douglas Haig, 1914–1919*, pp. 97–98.

[84] *Ibid.*, p. 109.

[85] The opinion of Lord Esher, an influential private adviser to the King. See Reginald Viscount Esher, *Journals and Letters*, III, 14. See also Harold Nicolson, *King George V*, p. 319.

[86] The judgment of Lord Beaverbrook, *Men And Power, 1917–1918*, p. 203. Beaverbrook's chapter, "All The King's Men," (pp. 186–216) considers the political position of Lloyd George in his dispute with the generals. It is examined throughout Paul Guinn's excellent study, *British Strategy and Politics, 1914–1918*.

[87] John Terraine, *The Great War 1914–1918*, p. 284.

[88] The conference and Haig's response to it are described in Robert Blake, ed., *The Private Papers of Douglas Haig, 1914–1919*, pp. 198–212. See also Paul Guinn, *British Strategy And Politics, 1914–1918*, pp. 214–17, and Harold Nicolson, *King George V*, pp. 302–06.

[89] Robert Blake, ed., *The Private Papers of Douglas Haig, 1914–1919*, pp. 208–09.

[90] Lord Stamfordham's memo on this interview is reproduced in Lord Beaverbrook, *Men And Power, 1917–1918*, pp. 412–14.

[91] Quoted in Lord Beaverbrook, *Men And Power, 1917–1918*, pp. 53.

[92] Kingsley Martin, *The Crown and the Establishment*, p. 82.

[93] Sir Ivor Jennings, *The British Constitution*, p. 113.

[94] Robert Blake, *The Unknown Prime Minister*, p. 460.

[95] When Churchill resigned in April 1955, there was no doubt the Queen would call Sir Anthony Eden. Still, Churchill insisted that there should be a one-day interval between his resignation and Eden's summons. This, he thought, would preserve the reality of the royal prerogative, a matter he thought very important. This was revealed by Harold Macmillan in the London *Times*, March 28, 1969. When Eden resigned in 1957 Elizabeth II was confronted with a problem very similar to the one faced by George V in 1923. Eden declined to recommend a successor and R. A. Butler and Harold Macmillan emerged as rivals for his position.

[96] Robert Blake, *The Unknown Prime Minister*, pp. 506–34, has a full account of this episode.

[97] Harold Nicolson, *King George V*, p. 376.

[98] Robert Cecil to King George V, November 1921. Major A. Hardinge, the King's Assistant Private Secretary, to Robert Cecil, November 15, 1921. Letters in the Robert Cecil Papers, MSSS. 51163, British Museum, London.

[99] Robert Blake, *The Unknown Prime Minister*, pp. 506–34.

[100] See Robert Rhodes James, ed., *Memoirs of a Conservative*, pp. 148–66. But in his latest study Robert Blake again argues that Waterhouse, whatever his motives, misrepresented Bonar Law. The unsigned memorandum prepared by Davidson was a much stronger and decisive recommendation of Baldwin than Law was prepared to make. Yet Lord Stamfordham was let to believe it "practically expressed the views of Mr. Bonar Law." However, Blake does not think the memorandum affected the outcome. Stamfordham actually recommended Lord Curzon but the King, in line with the advice of Arthur Balfour, sent for Baldwin because he was in the House of Commons and appeared to be the candidate

favored by the Parliamentary party. (See *The Conservative Party from Peel to Churchill*, pp. 211–13.)

[101] Reginald Bassett, *Nineteen Thirty-One* gives the fullest account of this episode. See also Harold Nicolson, *King George V*, pp. 444–69, and Charles Loch Mowat, *Britain Between The Wars, 1918–1940*, pp. 379–412.

[102] W. Ivor Jennings, "The Constitution Under Strain," *Political Quarterly*, April–June 1932, p. 196.

[103] Cited in Ivor Bulmer-Thomas, *The Growth of the British Party System*, II, 59.

[104] James Pope-Hennessy, *Queen Mary, 1867–1953*, p. 550.

[105] Herbert Viscount Samuel, *Grooves of Change*, p. 266, and Harold Nicolson, *King George V*, p. 461. Nicolson gives the testimony of the King's private secretary on the influence of Samuel: "It was after the King's interview with Sir Herbert Samuel that His Majesty became convinced of the necessity for the National Government."

[106] Cited in Reginald Bassett, *Nineteen Thirty-One, p. 365.*

[107] James Pope-Hennessy, *Queen Mary, 1867–1953*, p. 548.

[108] Herbert Morrison, *Herbert Morrison*, p. 128.

[109] The constitutional case against the King was made by Harold Laski, *The Crisis and the Constitution: 1931 and After*, and more briefly by Leonard Woolf, "A Constitutional Revolution," *Political Quarterly*, October-December 1931, pp. 475–77. Their arguments are rehearsed and refined by Graeme Moodie, "The Monarch and the Selection of a Prime Minister: A Re-Examination of the Crisis of 1931," *Political Studies*, February 1957, pp. 1–20. But see Reginald Bassett's rebuttal in *Nineteen Thirty-One*, pp. 358–75, 393–407.

[110] Herbert Viscount Samuel, *Grooves of Change*, p. 246.

[111] Reginald Bassett, *Nineteen Thirty-One*, pp. 370–75, makes a convincing case against such a constitutional limitation. See also John W. Wheeler-Bennett, *A Wreath to Clio*, p. 15, who says that in the appointment of a prime minister "Full power and responsibility . . . remain with the sovereign in the case of a national emergency necessitating the formation of a national or coalition government."

[112] Herbert Morrison, *Herbert Morrison*, pp. 128–30; Herbert Morrison, *Government and Parliament*, second edition, pp. 77–80; and Graeme Moodie, "The Monarch And The Selection of A Prime Minister: A Re-Examination of the Crisis of 1931," *Political Studies*, February 1957, pp. 1–20. Says Morrison in *Government and Parliament*: "As I see it, the King had unwittingly become involved in . . . an unnecessary and unpleasant political manoeuvre by Mr. MacDonald and his allies, calculated to inflict grave injury on the Labour Party and to benefit the Conservatives—as it did."

[113] For an interesting discussion of this practice see S. K. Panter-Brick, "Constitutional Monarch: a Comment On A Belgian Practice," *The Cambridge Journal*, July 1954, pp. 601–14.

[114] The sole exception came in 1921 with the opening of the new Ulster Parliament, when the King pressed the Government to allow him to make a personal appeal for forbearance and conciliation among all Irishmen. His ministers readily agreed. See Harold Nicolson, *King George V*, pp. 352–54.

[115] Harold Nicolson, *King George V*, p. 510.

[116] Sir Ernest Barker, "The Movement of National Life, 1910–1935," *The Fortnightly*, May 1935, p. 513.

[117] See James Pope-Hennessy, *Queen Mary*, pp. 430–31.

CHAPTER 4

THE CONTEMPORARY MONARCHY

George V had set exacting standards for monarchy, and some doubted if the Prince of Wales, who took the name of Edward VIII, could meet them. One of the doubters was the old King himself, who shortly before his death told his Prime Minister: "After I am dead the boy will ruin himself within twelve months."[1] That fear was borne out; Edward was King for less than a year. Had he remained on the throne he would have worked many changes in his inheritance. As it was, the Duke of York, who possessed many of the qualities of his father, immediately revived the name and character of the Georgian monarchy.

At his accession Edward VIII appeared well equipped to continue the traditions of democratic kingship. Hailed as "the most universally popular personality in the world," Edward's personal charm, so reminiscent of Edward VII, had already dazzled millions. As described by a journalist in 1926:

> His presence and his address are both attractive. Slight of figure—he weighs only 9.2 stone—he keeps himself in perfect physical condition by rigorous exercises, and watches any tendency to increase in weight with the anxiety of a jockey. His spirits are high, his smile instant and responsive, and his manner boyish and impulsive and entirely free from any calculated restraints . . . If his intellectual gifts are not remarkable, they are sufficient. He has the natural bonhomie which warms the ceremonial air, and he can deliver a speech as gallantly as he can ride a horse.[2]

As a goodwill ambassador for Britain the Prince had made triumphant tours of the Dominions, India, South America, and parts of the United States and the Orient. His infectious enthusiasm and easy manner had captivated every audience. George V, as well as British and Commonwealth statesmen, had praised his flair for public sympathy, and at his accession the *Times* wrote of the remarkable spell he had cast "upon the imagination of the many communities within what is henceforth his realm."[3] Edward had clearly demonstrated that he possessed the public presence so essential for the "field work" of monarchy.

To complete the almost story-book image of the Prince came accounts of the sensitive nature of the man. An example was his visit to a hospital ward of soldiers blinded in the First World War. He was so overcome by what he saw that he was unable to speak. And in 1936, during a tour of the depressed areas of South Wales, he was reported to have suddenly exclaimed: "Terrible, terrible, something will be done about this."[4] Other incidents of a similar nature were given wide public circulation, and cited as proof of his "warm sympathy and sincere regard for his fellowmen."[5]

Edward's youthfulness—he himself noted that at 41 he was the first monarch of the century who had not spent half of his life under the shadow of Victoria—was also welcomed by some as an asset for monarchy in 1936. It was the year the European Fascists went on the offensive with the Rhineland crisis, the conquest of Abyssinia and the Civil War in Spain. Perhaps the King, as a contrast to his aging ministers—Baldwin (69) and Chamberlain (67)—would do something to reverse Britain's image in the Fascist countries as a tired and complacent democracy. The impatient also hoped that Edward would ginger up his government, and a few of his public statements did lend credence to the popular view that he was pressing his ministers to take more decisive action at home on social questions, and abroad in working for the pacification of Europe. The royal remarks annoyed the politicians, but enhanced the King's public reputation as a man of spirit who possessed a manner of refreshing directness.

Only a few nagging doubts showed through the general euphoria as Edward ascended the throne. There was his marital status. Although the Prince had had his infatuations, and rumor had linked his name to several eligible princesses, he had advanced into middle age without a consort. This meant that the royal residences could not be the center of family feeling in the country. How would this affect the representation of monarchy as the living ideal of family life? A second worry was related to the first. Edward had created his own ethos as the fun-loving and restless Prince Charming. With his changed status would he settle down and become more serious, or would it soon become apparent that the King and the Prince were the same man?

Private misgivings about the King, held by the Court, the Foreign Office and the Government, ran even deeper. These were created by Edward's disregard for the pattern of kingship fashioned by his father: the strict respect for constitutional proprieties, and the fulfillment of the dignified functions of monarchy according to the Georgian prescription. Doubts were also based on knowledge of the King's character and social life, neither of which satisfied those who admired the Georgian monarchy. Gradually the misgivings hardened into resentments, and finally alarm, but they were carefully screened from the public, which did not learn that its

Prince Charming had faults until the news of the King's attachment to Mrs. Simpson was revealed to the country.

Some tension between the new monarch and his Court was inescapable: They represented different generations, and they differed on the philosophy of kingship. Court officials were loyal to the Georgian conception of royalty, and convinced of its unique success. They had witnessed the great outpouring of affection for King George and Queen Mary in 1935, and the deep grief following the death of the King in 1936. It was natural that they should believe that the nation was endorsing a style of public and private behavior in royalty, and that any fundamental departure from it was a mark of folly, as well as of disrespect.

But Edward was conscious of his own personality and success, and accustomed to running his own show as Prince of Wales. He was not about to school himself to a pattern shaped by a father whose habits, tastes and views were a reflection of the Victorian age. Open to new experiences, and affected by the restlessness which marked many of his generation, the Prince was even in rebellion against old standards. He believed that it was his mission to modernize the monarchy, to "throw open the windows" and allow fresh air into the "venerable institution."[6] It should become more human and less distant, which meant the monarch should be more relaxed and informal, less pompous and majestic.

In reforming the monarchy Edward followed no blueprint or conscious design, but it was clear that he meant to stamp his own personality on it. His first radio address to the country struck an informal and personal note and set the tone for his reign:

> I am better known to most of you as the Prince of Wales—as a man who, during the War and since, has had the opportunity of getting to know the people of nearly every country of the world, under all conditions and circumstances. And, although I now speak to you as the King, I am still the same man who has had that experience and whose constant effort it will be to continue to promote the well-being of his fellow men.[7]

Certainly Edward was better prepared to mix with his subjects on a more informal footing than any of his predecessors: His freer upbringing had enabled him to rub shoulders with all manner of people at Naval College, at Oxford, on the war front, and on his world-wide tours. Unlike his father, he also understood and sympathized with the modern tendencies.

A more democratic education, however, also made Edward feel less royal. He discovered that his interests and desires were similiar to those of others, and he experienced a longing to be treated as an ordinary person.[8] George V had admonished the Prince to "always remember your position and who you are"[9] but instead Edward grew cynical about his elevated status, and less comfortable in the role he was expected to fill. When invested with great pomp as Prince of Wales at Caenarvon Castle in 1911, for example, Edward found the ceremony uncongenial, even absurd. He felt foolish wearing white satin breeches and a mantle and surcoat of purple velvet edged with ermine. He fretted about what his fellow naval cadets would think of him, and little comforted by a sympathetic mother who advised, "Your friends will understand that as a Prince you are obliged to do certain things that may seem a little silly. It will be only for this once."[10] Edward also grew skeptical of the value of pomp and pageantry. In 1914, while at Oxford, he recorded his disgust about the time, money and energy spent preparing for the state visit of the King and Queen of Denmark. It was all "unreal show and ceremony."[11] Edward always disliked formal dress, and in private life wore "Robinson Crusoe" clothes. In his garden he pottered about in old trousers and a sweat shirt; on his sea holidays he wore shorts and sandals—at times, to the horror of his friends and attendants, in full view of onlookers.[12] Accordingly, the Prince as King could be expected to cut back on some of the pomp and pageantry to which Edward VII and George V had been so devoted.

Court officials also doubted whether Edward's temperament was entirely suitable for the duller aspects of kingship. His parents found him fidgety as a child; as Prince of Wales he had puzzled and vexed his father by his "reckless desire for change."[13] He preferred company where there was no "tedious standing on ceremony."[14] Would he, then, attend to his desk work and state papers? Would he bear patiently with the tedious protocol of monarchy? In fact, Edward did find paper work and public ceremony irksome and tried to curtail both. The royal household and civil servants concluded, as a result, that he "dislikes work and escapes from it and postpones its performance."[15] Edward, however, was convinced that what was at stake was his right to be King "in terms of my own philosophy."[16] He was angry and puzzled by opposition to his efforts to shed some of the layers of protocol around the throne. The Court functionaries resisted even "modest innovations," recalls the Duchess of Windsor. "Even I, remote as I was from the Court, could feel their cold, serried resentment."[17]

Court officials of course doubted the wisdom of Edward's philosophy, believing as they did that the essence of monarchy was dignity and mystery. They cited Bagehot as an authority: "He [the monarch] should not be brought too closely to real measurement. He should be aloof and solitary."[18] And how, they wondered, could majesty be retained, and the ceremonial role carry conviction, when the person who was to act the royal part rode a bronco in Canada, hit a golf ball off the Great Pyramid of Giza, rode a surf canoe along the Gold Coast, and walked to work in London?

The differing approaches to kingship were summed up in 1919 in a conversation between the Prince and Sir Frederick Ponsonby, Keeper of the Privy Purse. Edward, who had solicited the old courtier's opinion on his performance as Prince of Wales, reproduced the exchange in his memoirs:

'If I may say so, Sir, I think there is a risk in your making yourself too accessible,' he [Ponsonby] answered unhesitatingly.

'What do you mean?' I asked.

'The Monarchy must always retain an element of mystery. A Prince should not show himself too much. The Monarchy must remain on a pedestal.'

I maintained otherwise, arguing that because of the social changes brought about by the war one of the most important tasks of the Prince of Wales was to bring the institution nearer the people.

'If you bring it down to the people,' Fritz Ponsonby said coldly, 'it will lose its mystery and influence.' 'I do not agree,' I said. 'Times are changing.' He replied severely, 'I am older than you are, sir; I have been with your father, your grandfather, and your great-grandmother. They all understood. You are quite mistaken.'[19]

Such differences did not make for a happy Court. Edward, who resented criticism, did not take his father's advisers into his confidence. And the royal household was convinced that Edward showed insufficient respect for the traditions of royalty. The Archbishop of Canterbury expressed the apprehension of George V's old courtiers when, after his first interview with Edward VIII, he wrote: "There is not only a new reign but a new regime. I can only be most thankful for what has been, and for what is to be, hope for the best. God guide the King."[20]

The style of the new regime also ruffled government, party and civil service officials. At the beginning of the reign the Prime Minister, Stanley Baldwin, lavished conventional tributes on the new monarch, but privately he conceded that he was nervous about Edward,[21] a feeling shared by a number of his colleagues. "I have felt all through," Neville Chamberlain was soon to confide to his diary, "that we should never be safe with this K[ing]."[22] J.C.C. Davidson later claimed that very early he had had "grave doubts whether the Prince of Wales would ever succeed to the throne (or that he would) become an adequate King of England."[23]

Edward's attitude and manner contrasted too much with those of his father to please the Government. George V sought the confidence of his Ministers, and had always parted with them reluctantly; Edward had little sympathy for his Ministers, whom he dismissed as old-fashioned and conventional. The father had had a perfect sense of his limitations; the son "knew little and interfered much."[24] George V had become fully reconciled to his restricted political role; Edward was impatient of "duty without decision, service without responsibility, pomp without power."[25] The old King had avoided friction whenever possible; Edward did not hesitate to criticize and provoke scenes. The politicians, in short, had been comfortable with George V, and were distinctly uncomfortable with his son.

The working relationship that the two monarchs had with their Ministers was probably determined by their differing approaches to authority. George V, schooled in the Navy, backed his Ministers, even Lloyd George, because they were in office. "His attitude was very much that of the quarterdeck," J.C.C. Davidson later speculated, "anyone who questioned the Captain was next-door to being a rebel."[26] But Edward had suffered at the hands of an authoritarian father, and tended to challenge the man in command. The politicians found him, in return, obstinate and willful. As a result Edward had little personal rapport with his Ministers, and it is doubtful if he exercised much influence in Government. To do so, he needed the respect and trust of his Ministers, which he did not have. Moreover, the monarch must use tact, which Edward did not possess. He even appeared to delight in irritating his Ministers by making public statements he knew would displease them.

It certainly was not Edward's politics which disturbed the Government in 1936: The King's outlook was scarcely distinguishable from the average Tory in Parliament. Nor did he promote a comprehensive social program: "I was certainly no cosmic thinker, with a blueprint for remaking Britain."[27] Ministers were unhappy with Edward's work habits, his tactlessness and indiscretions. According to Baldwin's biographers:

> The King combined a somewhat desultory manner of dealing with official boxes with strong views on his right to intervene in affairs of state. Where foreign policy was concerned, the King did not disguise his opinions and attempted to enforce them on the government in a manner unknown for over a century.[28]

Court officials, cabinet members and civil servants complained of Edward's laziness in reading state papers and in doing his official work. Apparently he did not do his boxes promptly, except in an early rush of energy which soon passed.[29] It is clear that he did not have George V's sense of duty, or his "almost fanatical sense of punctuality."[30] Routine business, too, became an even greater burden when it kept Edward from Mrs. Simpson. "Before her," reported the King's private secretary, "the affairs of state sank into insignificance."[31]

Of much greater concern, however, was Edward's inclination—in disregard of settled practice—to intervene in affairs of state. He had no sympathy for the tradition of an apolitical monarchy, and was determined to exert himself on matters of national importance. In 1936 two issues—unemployment and Anglo-German relations—troubled many Englishmen, and received the attention of the King.

The depressed economy of the interwar years, and the human anguish it created, disturbed both George V and Edward VIII. They frequently toured depressed industrial areas, and talked to representatives of the army of the unemployed (at least 1,200,000 or more than 10 per cent of the nation's insured labor force were out of work every year of the 1920s and 1930s). Both men were moved and shocked by the plight of their unemployed subjects, and eager to encourage remedial activity. But they faced the dilemma of those who had service without responsibility. So major an economic and human problem as mass unemployment was inevitably a sensitive political problem. How, then, could the monarchy focus attention on the problem, and generate concern for the unemployed, and still remain politically neutral? Its activities must not ruffle the Government, but at the same time it must not allow ministers to take shelter behind the royal purple, and use the Crown to neutralize political discontent.[32]

George V coped with this dilemma better than his son. He used the normal cushions of protocol to protect himself against gaffes, and yet his sympathy and good will were not obscured. Edward's direct manner and frequent disregard of traditional ceremony made royal indiscretions more likely. Moreover, he refused to avoid sensitive domestic issues, viewing it as his duty "to intervene in the economic system" when it appeared to bring distress to the working classes.[33] He was undisturbed when his off-the-cuff remarks about housing and unemployment problems implied a censure of his Ministers and caused sensations in the country. His most publicized intervention came in November 1936, when he toured the depressed mining areas of South Wales in company with Ernest Brown, the Minister of Labour. He expressed horror and surprise at the conditions he observed and promised something would be done, comments which were picked up by the popular press and interpreted as an indictment of a complacent government. "The man in the street," said the *Daily News*, "feels that Whitehall stands condemned."[34]

These incidents did no harm to Edward's popularity in the country. Here was a monarch, it was said in the pubs, who would not take any nonsense from Baldwin.[35] But political leaders, Labour no less than Conservative, deplored the King's behavior. " . . . I did not think well of it," Herbert Morrison later wrote, "for it was a case of a sovereign publicly expressing views on matters which were the subject of political controversy."[36] Monarchs were natural Tories, and so even Labour, although it appreciated Edward's concern for the unemployed, had every reason to insist that monarchy play by the traditional rules.

Edward also assumed a lively and active role in foreign affairs, which was not welcomed by Anthony Eden, the young Foreign Minister, or the Foreign Office. He was, says one of Eden's biographers, "an impetuous and often opinionated man who did not understand the limits imposed on a modern monarch, and lacked his father's intimate knowledge of foreign affairs."[37] Indeed, George V had rebuked the Prince several times for making statements without the prior approval of the Foreign Office.

The King's outlook on foreign affairs was not unconventional, but the manner in which he pressed his views upon the Government was. He favored a strong navy, an accelerated program of rearmament, and a foreign policy based on "realism," not the League of Nations, which he dismissed as a "will-o'-the-wisp" body. He opposed the use of League sanctions against Italy for its invasion of Abyssinia, and declined to receive Haile Selassie at Buckingham Palace when the Emperor fled to England. Such a gesture would be unpopular with the Italians, the King told Eden, who had urged it. His Ministers "had embarked upon a futile policy of coercing Mussolini," he later wrote. " I could see no point in indulging in half-measures that could not succeed. It was more important in my eyes at this stage to gain an ally than to score debating victories in the tottering League of Nations."[38]

Always a strong Germanophile, Edward also worked for greater Anglo-German harmony. He received German delegations, encouraged the exchange of visits between ex-servicemen from the two countries, and attended a dinner at the German Embassy in July 1935. He also embraced the widely-held notion that Berlin was justified in demanding revisions in the Versailles settlement. When Germany made a unilateral and illegal adjustment of the 1919 arrangements—the occupation of the demilitarized zone of the Rhineland on March 7, 1936—Edward urged the British Government not to resist. Apparently he intervened with Baldwin at the express request of the German ambassador, von Hoesch. An intimate of the ambassador, who was present when the King made a telephone reply, later wrote of the conversation:

> Von Hoesch whispered to me: "The King!" and handed the second receiver to me, so that I could listen to the conversation.
> "Hullo," a voice called, "is that Leo? David speaking. Do you know who's speaking?"
> "Of course I do," replied von Hoesch.
> "I sent for the Prime Minister and gave him a piece of my mind. I told the old so-and-so that I would abdicate if he made war. There was a frightful scene. But you needn't worry. There won't be a war."[39]

This story is not confirmed by other evidence, but it is not out of character with Edward's public statements. Baldwin's biographers, who are inclined to accept the account, suggest that Baldwin would have agreed with the King that there should be no war, but "he could not have tolerated his [Edward's] action in bringing pressure to bear upon his Ministers."[40] They maintain that because of the King's work habits, and his propensity for indiscretions, all Foreign Office papers sent to the King were carefully checked to see that nothing highly secret could go astray. Mrs. Simpson was regarded with open suspicion. A political innocent, she accepted party and luncheon invitations at the German Embassy, and was reportedly a personal friend of Herr von Ribbentrop, who became the German ambassador in London in October 1936. The security services kept watch on her and some of her friends.[41]

Because of his pronounced German bias, Edward was regarded as a fascist sympathizer in certain circles. Some Labourites who might normally have sided with the King on the issue of Mrs. Simpson, declined to do so because of the allegedly pro-fascist slant of his public statements.[42] Jessica Mitford paraded in front of Buckingham Palace in support of the King and Mrs. Simpson, but admits in her autobiography that she had doubts about the King's politics at the time. "Edward had recently shown signs of being

impressed with Hitler's regime."[43] Nor did Edward's conduct after the abdication serve to discount these suspicions. In October 1937 he toured
Germany under the auspices of a pro-Nazi, and had a personal interview
with Hitler. In the spring of 1939 he disregarded the advice of the British
Government and made a world-wide broadcast for peace. Hitler himself
believed that Edward was favorably inclined to his regime and it is said that
he had plans to restore him to the throne after a successful invasion of
England.[44]

The rumors of Edward's fascist sympathies were false; he was no
admirer of Hitler. Their very existence, however, stood as proof of the
King's political limitations, and of the dangers of his activist philosophy.
Edward, as Victoria before him, must be faulted on political judgment.
His influence in private was slight; his interventions in public counter-
productive, even dangerous for the Crown. This was the wrong formula
for constitutional monarchy and it is fortunate for the country and the
Crown that his successor reverted to the safer constitutional behavior of
George V.

Contrary to claims found in a few published accounts of Edward's abdication, however, his departure was not linked directly to the dissatis-
faction caused by his performance in politics. It was charged that Baldwin
and his colleagues conspired to remove the King because he refused to
play by the rules of his father.[45] Lord Beaverbrook's political narrative,
published posthumously in 1966, reiterated this thesis: "The movement to
deprive King Edward VIII of his royal inheritance was launched at the outset of his reign, before he had declared his love for Mrs. Simpson."[46] Cabinet Members certainly thought Edward ill-suited for his job, but there is no
evidence that they ever plotted to get rid of him. The pressures leading to
the King's abdication were created by Edward's decision, maintained in the
face of all official advice, to marry Mrs. Simpson. It was this crisis over the
King's dignified role which sealed his fate.

The matter of the King's marriage immediately fused the private and
public behavior of monarchy in a dramatic fashion. As Baldwin pointed
out " . . . the position of the King's wife was different from the position of
the wife of any other citizen in the country: it was part of the price which
the King has to pay. His wife becomes Queen; the Queen becomes the
Queen of the country; and therefore, in the choice of a Queen, the voice
of the people must be heard."[47] In a strict constitutional sense the King
could marry anyone he wished without official advice as long as she was
not a Roman Catholic, but Edward appreciated the public nature of the
act, and the wisdom of obtaining official approval. Should the Government
disapprove it might resign and thereby involve the Crown in politics. It
represented another of those unwritten erosions of the royal prerogative.

As the affair unfolded, it became clear that Edward had committed two
major errors of judgment. First, he did not foresee, or make any provision
to offset, the extensive opposition encountered. "It shows the political limitations of the Prince," says Lewis Broad, "that he made no plans in readiness for the clash that lay ahead."[48] Second, Edward failed to perceive how

public had become all aspects of royal life. Twentieth-century monarchs had unwittingly made this inevitable: The emphasis upon dignified functions made it virtually impossible to lead a private life quite distinct from the public and formal.

The development was most clearly seen in the notion that the royal family represented an ideal domesticity. To be a devoted family man, Edward himself later wrote, went a long way for a King in a constitutional monarchy. This ideal domestic life might not apply to Edward at his accession because he was a bachelor, the first unmarried King to come to the throne since George III in 1760. But when he did choose a consort it was expected that she should correspond to the public ideal of a Queen.

Another development—mass communications—also tended to diminish the sphere of privacy for royalty. Edward received more exposure than any other heir apparent in history as the popular press lavished attention and praise on him, as radio beamed his voice to millions, and as the cinema carried his image around the world. All this involved a new burden and responsibility. The public appetite for news grew, and royalty found the mass media digging up and broadcasting the smallest details about their lives. But this vast exposure also gave the royal family great moral influence, and called for a new technique of royalty, "a technique of living with integrity and domestic simplicity under the never-extinguished arc lamps of publicity."[49]

One of Edward's reforms, however, was to carve out more privacy for the monarch. He insisted that his private life was his own; his new status as King would not alter his former social habits or circle of friends. His advisers undoubtedly wished to impose new restrictions upon him; these he would not tolerate. Nor did he wish to take up residence in Buckingham Palace, preferring to remain at Fort Belvedere near Windsor, which he called his "Get-Away-from-People house."[50] Here he would relax in the company of a few intimate friends drawn from a small world of well-dressed and amusing cosmopolitans. His dancing partners, at the Fort and in London, were frequently married women.

Certainly George V had not approved of his son's parties and company. And it was knowledge of Edward's private life, even more than his public indiscretions, that raised doubts in the minds of court and public officials about his ability to face the responsibilities of kingship. Aristocratic society, for its part, was contemptuous of this "Cafe Society," which it claimed was turning the royal residences into American night clubs.[51] The British press was far more discreet about the King's social activities and friends than the American and European newspapers, however, and so they did not fall under the domestic arc lamps of publicity until December 1936. Press revelations then shocked the country, or at least the provinces, which were much more puritan than London. Even without the Simpson episode it is doubtful if Edward could have continued to lead a private life so at variance with the standards set by his father and still avoid public criticism.

But it was Edward's attachment to Mrs. Simpson which first convinced the country of the King's inability to uphold the dignified functions of monarchy. Wallis Simpson, who was first introduced to the Prince in 1930, was the first "to penetrate the heart of his inner loneliness, his sense of separateness"[52] and to offer him spiritual companionship. Edward also found her comments "deft and and amusing" and her interest in his work flattering.[53] He became deeply devoted to her, resolving in 1934 that she must become his wife. He came to the throne then, with "his life and activities . . . already dedicated to a secret hope."[54] But that secret was not officially communicated to his family or the Government until November 1936.

Even the sturdiest enemies of the Simpson marriage confessed she had great charm. Geoffrey Dawson of the *Times* thought her "pleasant, quiet and sensible."[55] Samuel Hoare, a more friendly observer, described her as "very attractive and intelligent."[56] She was "polished and sophisticated," writes the photographer Cecil Beaton, wore clothes of "smartly modernistic aspect" and belonged to "the world of restaurants and drawing-rooms."[57] This was all very well, of course, but whatever her attractions as a person Mrs. Simpson was certainly not another Queen Mary. She had almost every disadvantage as a royal consort—she was an American, she was married, and she had a divorced first husband still living. But in spite of these formidable handicaps Edward was certain something could be worked out; Mrs. Simpson was in "a dreamy state of happy and unheeding acceptance."[58]

After he came to the throne Edward did nothing to hide his affections. In fact, he paraded his passion before the world most indiscreetly. At a royal dinner party in July Mrs. Simpson, unaccompanied by her husband, even joined such select guests as the Duke and Duchess of York, Sir Samuel and Lady Hoare, and the Prime Minister and his wife.[59] Social circles buzzed with rumors about an impending marriage, but it seemed so incredible that only a few really took the reports seriously. That is, not until events of the summer and fall gave substance to what before was regarded only as gossip. In August and early September Edward and Mrs. Simpson vacationed aboard the *Nahlin* in the Mediterranean and along the Dalmatian coast. Seen everywhere together and cheered as lovers by excited sightseers, they were trailed by a troop of journalists and photographers. American readers were deluged with sensational stories about the King and his "girl friend," but with few exceptions the British press, by voluntary agreement, did not comment on what was a spicy topic of conversation and speculation elsewhere. Back in London Mrs. Simpson filed for divorce in October, and this gave added reason to believe Edward was serious. Should the divorce be granted, it would leave her free to marry the King shortly before the coronation in May 1937. It was this information, together with reports of the deleterious effect sensational stories in the foreign press were having on the prestige of Britain and its monarchy, which prompted Baldwin to intervene with some fatherly advice for his monarch.[60]

The roles of the two parties were now strangely reversed: it was the Prime Minister, not the King, who asked to be consulted, who encouraged a different behavior, and who offered warnings. And it was the Prime Minister, backed by his Cabinet, the opposition parties, the church and the Dominion governments, who insisted that he knew far better than Edward what the country demanded of their monarch.

Perhaps morals had gone to pieces since the war, Baldwin told the King on October 20, but "it only leads the people to expect a higher standard from their King. . . . " He then tried to persuade Edward to mend his ways, beginning by sending Mrs. Simpson out of the country.[61] At no time during his first session with the King did Baldwin even utter the word marriage. Instead he spoke of his anxieties and of the harm Edward's conduct was having on the prestige of the Crown; apparently he hoped his warnings would sober the King and lead him to end his relationship with Mrs. Simpson voluntarily. In this Baldwin was too optimistic; blunter advice was necessary, but his very reluctance to raise the question of marriage weakens the argument that the Prime Minister wished to force Edward off the throne.

Undoubtedly Baldwin was right about public expectations. Time was to suggest that at least in the provinces people had very definite notions about the dignified functions of monarchy, which Edward was to offend. As an observer for Mass-Observation reported from a Gloucestershire village during George VI's coronation: "They all seemed to feel George VI is like his father—a safe King. Villagers do not approve of any irregularity in their Royal Family."[62]

In subsequent sessions with the King, Baldwin warned him that the Government—and he thought opinion in the country and Empire—would never consent to have Mrs. Simpson as Queen. The King was, after all, Defender of the Faith, and the church disapproved of the remarriage of divorced persons. And beyond the church a formidable puritanism still existed, as Edward and Parliament were to discover. Nor did belated attempts to promote a morganatic marriage make any impression on those opposed to the Simpson marriage. The cabinet turned the proposal down, as did the Dominion governments.[63] The *Times* expressed their view in that famous sentence: "The Constitution is to be amended in order that she may carry in solitary prominence the brand of unfitness for the Queen's throne."[64] Ellen Wilkinson, a popular Socialist Member of Parliament, expressed the same view somewhat less elegantly: "We are not going to acknowledge two sorts of women, one a wife, but a wife not good enough to be Queen."[65]

Edward, however, disputed Baldwin's claim to have the pulse of the nation. He was not, after all, a Gallup poll. He was certain that his personal popularity could withstand any strain caused by his unconventional match; if properly explained, it would be endorsed by the great warm heart of the people. When he announced on November 16, "I mean to marry her and I am prepared to go," therefore, Edward was probably only using shock tactics in order to bring his Ministers to heel.[66] When even his morganatic proposal was rejected by the Cabinet and the Dominion governments, he sought a direct appeal to the country. "Its purpose," he later wrote, "was to present my problem in its true light—not merely as a knotty and abstruse constitutional issue, but as a call of the heart. . . . "[67] The request was rejected as certain to divide the country.

So certain was Edward of his standing in the country and Empire that he even disregarded the advice of his private secretary, Alex Hardinge, a personal appointee who acted as "the eyes and ears" of the monarch. In a famous letter sent on November 13, Hardinge openly warned Edward of an impending crisis, one which could only be avoided by sending Mrs. Simpson abroad at once.[68] It was an anguished but common-sense letter which finally forced the King to make his position clear to the Government, which he did on November 16. Edward's response to the advice, however, is indicative of his stubbornness and imprudence: he was angry and resentful and refused thereafter to take his private secretary into his confidence.

Speculation on the measure of public support Edward might have aroused by a national appeal is really pointless. Monarchy must obviously claim almost universal support for its actions, and on this matter—as his unofficial and official advisers had warned—powerful groups were adamantly opposed to the King's proposed course. The House of Commons was overwhelmingly anti-King. Henry "Chips" Channon, a friend of Edward and Mrs. Simpson, was shocked to find that in the House "the monarchy has lost ground in a frightening manner. Prince Charming charms his people no more. . . . "[69] That shrewd observer, Harold Nicolson, thought the King had little sympathy from any segment of the population. When the crisis broke in the press on December 3 he was addressing a group at Islington. There was, he says, "a deep and enraged fury against the King," so that only about 10 out of 400 people in the congregation joined in singing the National Anthem.[70]

Baldwin had also sounded out Labour leaders. Clement Attlee informed him that Labour did not approve of the King's favor toward Mrs. Simpson, and Walter Citrine, the powerful trade union official, assured the Prime Minister that he was representing the attitude of the labor movement.[71] This outlook of the labor movement was, for some persons, of more decisive influence than the views of the Cabinet or Dominion premiers. J.C.C. Davidson has recorded:

> There was not the slightest doubt on the part of Attlee or Bevin that the only alternatives facing the King were renunciation of Mrs. Simpson or abdication. No compromise was possible. . . . Shortly before the crisis, a senior member of the Labour Party had attempted to make his mistress the official hostess at social functions at the Annual Party Conference. None of the wives of the leading members of the Party was prepared to shake her hand when she received the guests. This small episode emphasized the strong Puritanism on such matters within the Labour Party. It was impossible to conceive of any Labour or trade union leader tolerating Mrs. Simpson as a consort of the King. We were close friends both of the Attlees and the Bevins, and I never had any doubt whatever where they stood in the crisis. . . .

At the beginning, the first instinct of many Socialists was to side with the King, for they remembered his sympathy with the terrible problems of the unemployed. But as the crisis unfolded they took a very different view, and this was particularly noticeable among the trade unions, who had a most profound contempt for the "goings-on" and somewhat disreputable private lives of London society. The very thought of the King marrying a twice-divorced woman who had two ex-husbands alive shocked them to the core. . . ."[72]

Other influential groups from the Civil Service, the Privy Council, Free and Anglican churches and the British Legion, also suggested that the King's popularity could not outweigh the proposed marriage. Many were convinced that the King's conduct had already done no end of harm to the country's prestige.[73] All of these groups were angry at Edward for shirking his duty and "letting the whole side down" in the eyes of the world. "It seemed inconceivable to those who had made such sacrifices during the war," Queen Mary later wrote, "that you, as their King, refused a lesser sacrifice."[74]

The strength of this hostile opinion made compromise impossible. Baldwin handled the matter tactfully and sympathetically, but when Edward refused to renounce Mrs. Simpson, abdication was inevitable. When that issue was resolved Baldwin's chief aim was to avoid a prolonged crisis, which he feared would split the country and undermine the throne. "What I want, Sir," he told Edward on December 3, "is what you told me you wanted: to go with dignity, not dividing the country, and making things as smooth as possible for your successor."[75] The King's only alternative, should he chose to consider it, was to find another ministry. His private secretary had warned on November 13 that this was impossible, but a few persons encouraged Edward to fight it out. And the King did seek the advice of Lord Beaverbrook and Winston Churchill, both already known as bitter critics of Baldwin's leadership.

Churchill urged Edward to play a waiting game, giving time for his friends to rally public support and expose the bullying tactics of the Government.[76] Beaverbrook's strategy also rested on delay.[77] Edward should not press the issue until after his coronation, for by then the Simpson divorce would be final, Baldwin might have retired, and the King's popularity would be more firmly established. For reasons embedded in his own personality, however, Edward wanted the question settled immediately. It was "No marriage, no Coronation." Would Beaverbrook's strategy have worked? It is doubtful. Baldwin was succeeded by Neville Chamberlain, an altogether tougher and harsher man who had no sympathy for Edward. And the public outcry would surely have made the King's position highly untenable.

Beaverbrook was even optimistic when the crisis broke in December. He was persuaded Churchill could fuse Socialist, Liberal, and Conservative splinter groups into an all-party administration.[78] A few signs early in the crisis were favorable to the "King's Party." The Beaverbrook and Rothermere press championed a morganatic marriage. At least 40 Members of Parliament were sympathetic.[79] Two Fellows of All Souls, G.F. Hudson and A.L. Rowse, urged Hugh Dalton, the Chairman of the Labour Party, to seize upon the issue to bring Baldwin down.[80] In London small demonstrations organized by the Fascists shouted anti-Baldwin slogans. Oswald Mosley, leader of the British Union of Fascists, coined the phrase, "Stand by the King," and hastily compiled a list of Cabinet members in the expectation the King would call upon him to form a government.[81]

But the campaign pushed by these disparate groups soon collapsed. Over the weekend of December 5-6, Members of Parliament tested constituency opinion, and most of them found it hard against the King. "Every time I dipped into the bran-tub of provincial opinion during these days," said Hugh Dalton, "I pulled out a Puritan." Moreover, with each day of delay public opinion moved against the King. He thought women were more emphatic and bitter than the men.[82] On Monday, December 7, the voice of the provinces was heard in Parliament. When Churchill rose to plead for more time he was shouted down by an angry House. The "King's Party" was dead. The historian of the abdication concludes:

> The "King's Party," in fact, never had any real existence. The pro-king demonstrations, as Dalton claimed, "were only froth." Edward's impression that a multitude of the plain people stood waiting to be rallied to his side had been justified only so long as the issues were not clear—so long as it was believed that the King was being bullied by "them." But as soon as it was realized that he wanted to marry a twice-divorced American woman, the mood had changed. "It wouldn't have done," as a taxi driver told Kingsley Martin, "it wouldn't have done."[83]

Equally as important was Edward's refusal to offer the "King's Party" any encouragement. Beaverbrook noted sadly: "Our cock won't fight."[84] The King never believed Baldwin's version of the public mind but he declined to play politics, and deferred to the wishes of his Ministers. His cooperation turned the crisis into "a nine-day wonder." The news broke in the press on December 3; Edward signed the Instrument of Abdication on December 10; and early on December 12 he slipped out of the country, comforted by the thought that "love had triumphed over the exigencies of politics."[85]

In the postmortems that followed his departure, however, others arrived at different conclusions. Those who had never expected Edward to be a King in the class of his father now felt their judgment had been vindicated. To survive, monarchy must rest on dignity and duty, they argued; and Edward had shown too little of those qualities. They were not to find anything in Edward's subsequent career as Duke of Windsor to indicate they were wrong. They had the comfort, too, of seeing a number of the King's prominent allies repent and concede Baldwin had been right.[86]

It was also argued that Edward had never wished to be King, so that Mrs. Simpson, consciously or unconsciously, represented "escape from the prison house."[87] And the King was condemned for laying down a great trust for the sake of private happiness. In a broadcast to the nation on the Sunday after the abdication, the Archbishop of Canterbury said: "From God he had received a high and sacred trust. Yet by his own will he has abdicated—he has surrendered the trust. With characteristic frankness he has told us his motive. It was a craving for private happiness."[88] This criticism, in particular, angered the Duke. He did wish to be King, he retorted, but at the same time he needed the support of the woman he loved in order to carry the burdens of kingship.[89]

Even with a wife, however, it is doubtful if Edward would ever have found happiness as a constitutional monarch. He had always performed some royal duties grudgingly, and those responsibilities would surely have continued to frustrate him. In 1966 he described the royal role in these terms:

> Being a Monarch, whether man or woman in these egalitarian times, can surely be one of the most confining, the most frustrating, and over the duller stretches, the least stimulating jobs open to an educated, independent-minded person. Even a saint would on occasion find himself driven to exasperation by the taboos which invisibly and silently envelop a constitutional monarchy. This is not meant in disrespect. It is only the way it looked to me from the inside.[90]

Perhaps, then, as even friends of the Windsors have speculated,[91] a crisis would have arisen with or without Mrs. Simpson. At least it may be doubted if a longer reign would have pleased either Edward or his subjects.

On the King's choice of a royal consort most observers had no difficulty in offering a moral—it was inconceivable that a British monarch should even consider a divorcee. That she should become Queen was an eventuality "almost too horrible to contemplate."[92] The *Times* had first greeted the prospect as "incompatible with the Throne" and the *Daily Telegraph* viewed it as certain to "fatally compromise" the dignity of the Crown.[93] In the mood of the times these comments did not seem unduly stuffy or severe. Baldwin also thought Archbishop Lang was "the voice of Christian England" when he condemned a happiness sought "in a manner inconsistent with the Christian principles of marriage."[94]

In Lord Beaverbrook's reflections, on the other hand, Mrs. Simpson is offered as the victim of an ecclesiastical prejudice already in decay. The barriers against divorced persons, he argues, were soon to be swept away. Before long "not a trace of the ancient prejudice will remain."[95] To be sure, in our day the stigma of divorce is no longer as serious as it once was. Anthony Eden became Prime Minister, although a divorced and remarried man; it is inconceivable that this could have happened in the late nineteenth or early part of the twentieth century.

But it is important to realize that monarchy is not measured against the domestic standards of the average citizen. Women in particular identify with royalty and expect to find it idealizing their own domestic virtues. It was, then,

> ... because Edward VIII contemplated a kind of domesticity legitimate enough for lesser persons by the permitted standards of the age, but such as the great central body of public opinion could not idealize, that the national instinct rejected him.[96]

George V and George VI offered a family life more easily idealized, and this satisfied the public.

As shown earlier, Edward VIII also wished to curtail another basic feature of the Georgian monarchy—its splendor and ceremony. Pomp and pageantry are essential ingredients of the social and psychological monarchy, however, so Edward's reforms would probably have decreased the popularity of the institution. These matters were never put to the country in a formal referendum, of course, but the success of the Georgian synthesis, when revived in the person of George VI, would seem to indicate that this is what people want in the way of monarchy. This is the significance of the abdication crisis, in fact, and the reason it is treated above at some length; it confirms the great popularity of the Georgian synthesis.

Upon Edward's departure the monarchy was restored in great measure to the Georgian fashion. The Duke of York pointedly adopted the title "George VI," and surrounded himself with his father's old advisers. Those who were anxious to recycle the royal style played up the most trivial similarities between father and son: The King's handwriting and signature, the Archbishop of Canterbury observed, were virtually indistinguishable from those of George V.[97] Not surprisingly Edward's brief reign became, in retrospect, the "strange interlude."

This return to the ways of his father harmonized with the natural preferences of the new monarch. "The patterns of their lives were much the same," wrote the Duke of Windsor, "with the steady swing of habit taking them both year after year to the same places at the same time and with the same associates."[98] Those retreats were always within Britain, as the royal family once again inhabited their traditional residences of Buckingham Palace, Windsor, Sandringham, and Balmoral.

Court life became at once duller and more formal, although not as stiff as it had been under George V, when ladies were invariably required to wear full evening dress and long white gloves for dinner. Of Windsor under the new regime Lord Esher might have written as he had twenty-five years before: "It is all very home-like and simple. . . . " Dinner was served promptly at 8:30, followed by drinks for the men and gossip for the women, and "Good night" at 10:30.[99] Although infinitely duller now, the Court, with its more formal and serious tone, at once took on the dignity and solidness it had had under George V. Many in the country found this reassuring. Even some of Edward VIII's social circle welcomed the change. Life at the Fort had been "an operetta," said Diana Cooper after an evening at Windsor in 1937; "this is an institution."[100]

George VI fitted willingly enough into the Georgian pattern, but it still required a high degree of self-effacement. For a person who was shy and unambitious and had none of his brother's brilliant public gifts and high spirits, however, this was not a great trial. As a person the new King was

> uninteresting and unintellectual, but doubtless wellmeaning . . . he improved with the years. His natural shyness and an inferiority complex towards his eldest brother made him on the defensive. He had no wit, no learning, no humour, except of a rather school-boy brand. He was nervous, ill at ease, though slightly better after some champagne. He had no vices and few interests other than shooting. . . . [101]

Since the age of eight George had also fought to overcome a stammer, achieving only limited success. This physical handicap increased his nervousness, and at times was a source of embarrassment to those who listened to him. In 1945 Harold Nicolson wrote of the King's address to Parliament:

> He has a really beautiful voice and it is to be regretted that his stammer makes it almost intolerably painful to listen to him. It is as if one read a fine piece of prose written on a typewriter the keys of which stick from time to time and mar the beauty of the whole. It makes him stress the wrong word.[102]

George was very conscious of his limitations, and thus dreaded the prospect of a life in the limelight. But by accepting the Crown and for fifteen years doggedly fulfilling the duties associated with it, the King, although endowed with few natural talents, was to earn the respect of the country. The association once again of his family and the monarchy with the idea of unselfish devotion to public service was probably his greatest accomplishment.

Although he did not have Edward's personal gifts, George VI did return family life to court; and this was essential for a "repolishing" of monarchy. "Conversation Pieces"—simple and intimate scenes of the King, the Queen, and their two daughters—were immediately popular, as they usually are with royalty. James Gunn produced one of the most famous of these pieces in 1950, a painting of the royal family at tea at the Royal Lodge, Windsor. It sums up—as it was intended to do—the character of the Georgian monarchy: the family in a simple and dignified setting. The King, a cigarette in his hand, the Queen, pouring tea, and Princess Elizabeth are seated around a table. Princess Margaret is pushing back her chair. The props for this natural and homey scene are tasteful and elegant—gleaming silver, fine china, lace-edge tablecloth, and sober but rich rugs and paintings. There is, then, a balance between the august and the domestic, with royal simplicity set off by royal majesty. It is this blend which effectively "exalts the affection of the subject and gives intimacy to his loyalty."[103]

In making this representation of the royal family the King was fortunate in his consort, the former Lady Elizabeth Bowes-Lyon, youngest daughter of the Earl of Strathmore, whom he had married in 1923. The Queen had a personal charm and natural grace lacked by the King, with a special genius for putting people at their ease. "Pretty and engaging and natural," Queen Mary had written in 1923 of the person she and George V thought ideally suited for the Duke of York.[104] There is no doubt that she played an important, even indispensable, role in attaching public affection once again to the monarchy.

The King approached his political obligations with as much trepidation as he had the representational. He had in fact almost no preparation for the job, and claimed not to have seen a state paper before 1936. He "stood appalled at the volume and nature of the business which emerged day by day from their leather-clad despatch boxes. . . . "[105] He could call to his aid an able private secretary, Alexander Hardinge, however, as well as his own orderly mind and conscientious nature. He studied his boxes faithfully every day, thereby developing a professional competence on a wide range of topics. During the war the American ambassador found him "completely informed on the day to day progress of the armed forces and on any other subject that concerned his people."[106] On business matters the King was probably so meticulous that he wore himself out unnecessarily. Not surprisingly, the strain of office soon undermined his health, which had always been delicate.

George VI brought to politics decidedly Conservative prejudices. J.C.C. Davidson's description of George V's political outlook—"He was very right-wing and he knew where his friends really lay, and that the Conservative Party was the King's Party and a radical party was not"[107]—would certainly apply to the son. But he remained strictly neutral on political questions, and this enabled him to win the confidence of his Labour ministers. Socialist legislation encountered not a ripple of opposition from the Palace, an indication of how circumstances and attitudes had changed since the constitutional crisis of 1909–1911.

Experience, knowledge and cordial relations with his ministers allowed the King to exercise influence discreetly, but there is no evidence to suggest George VI played a significant role in the key decisions of the day. This does not mean that the King was completely passive, or that he failed to use his Bagehotian rights. Several incidents during George VI's reign reveal the King's influence in minor matters, and suggest the manner in which monarchs in modern times can exert themselves.

Although the affair is still wrapped in some mystery, there is reason to believe the King played an important role in the dismissal of Leslie Hore-Belisha from the War Office in January 1940. At the War Office since 1937, Hore-Belisha had aroused considerable resentment in the Army because of a number of reforms he had instituted and the assertive manner in which he carried them through. In 1939 there was also friction between the Minister and the British High Command in France. Elements within the General Staff managed to persuade the Duke of Gloucester, a professional soldier, to carry their case to his brother, the King. And the Army's views were also pressed upon George VI when he visited the Expeditionary Force in France in December 1939.

The King, who had a deep concern for army morale, and as great a respect for military opinion as his father, discussed the Army's criticisms of Hore-Belisha with the Prime Minister. Until then Chamberlain had sided with his Minister but shortly after he asked Hore-Belisha to resign because of "personal relations." In his resignation speech Hore-Belisha made only one oblique remark in which he implied that outside pressure was responsible for his eviction. Otherwise he remained silent. But Henry Channon, a personal friend of the Minister and of the Duke of Kent, was convinced that royal intervention had tipped the scales and decided the Minister's fate.[108]

It is doubtful if the King acted wisely in the affair. Hore-Belisha was a popular politician who had become identified in the public mind with efforts to democratize the Army. His dismissal was blamed on generals who wished to impede reforms in that direction. The King's intervention, had it become known, might have cheapened the Crown, undermined his own popularity, and impaired national unity. At the time George VI had not gained the affection and respect which the war effort, and his own role in it, were soon to give him. The wisdom of the King apart, however, the affair stands as an example of how the contemporary monarchy is able to affect important decision, especially when they involve the armed services.

Another occasion when George VI exercised his right to advise was in July 1945, when Clement Attlee called at the Palace to receive a commission to form a Government. Because the Potsdam Conference was pending, the King asked Attlee whom he had in mind for the Foreign Office. Attlee mentioned Hugh Dalton. The King disagreed and urged consideration of Ernest Bevin. As it turned out, Bevin did become Foreign Minister, and so the Palace assumed that the King's remark had shaped the outcome. But later Attlee did not even recall the King's advice, and he claimed that other factors had led him to change his mind and select Bevin. The Prime Minister, therefore, probably did not make his decision under royal influence, although the final appointment did coincide with the King's expressed hope. Nevertheless, this incident illustrates the manner in which a monarch can exercise private influence in government.[109]

The King's biographer relates a third case involving George VI and his Prime Minister. In the summer of 1945, the Labour Government introduced and carried a Supplies and Services Bill designed to give it special powers to deal with the economic crisis and to ensure continued supplies and services for the community. The press and the Opposition expressed alarm about the consequences of the Act: It might jeopardize individual rights, and enable the Government to bypass Parliament, and introduce a social revolution by Ministerial Order. These charges disturbed the King, and the controversy that swirled around the Bill distressed him. On August 26 he asked Attlee to "tell me what you yourself intended the purpose, and the scope of the Bill to be." Attlee replied in a long memorandum in which he justified the Bill, outlined its intended use, and assured the King that individual and parliamentary rights were not endangered.[110] This correspondence did not change anything, but it made the Government rethink the issue, and justify its position to the Crown.

And this was the role Bagehot projected for constitutional monarchy.

Only once did it appear that George VI might be called upon to exercise one of the Crown's special reserve powers. In February 1950, Attlee's Labour Government was narrowly returned to office, emerging from the election with a majority of eight in the Commons. Normally a Government must have a far larger cushion if it is to operate effectively, and so it was assumed that Attlee would soon be defeated and request another dissolution. This provoked a debate on the King's role and rights: Should he consent to an immediate second dissolution? Did he have the right to refuse, and if so, on what grounds? George V had thought he had the right to refuse a dissolution, although he never exercised it, and a number of constitutionalists in 1950 upheld this claim. A learned correspondence on the question took place in the columns of the *Times*. The King's private secretary, Sir Alan Lascelles, writing under a pseudonym, made his own contribution:[111]

> Sir:
>
> It is surely indisputable (and common sense) that a Prime Minister may ask—not demand—that his Sovereign will grant him a dissolution of Parliament; and that the Sovereign, if he so chooses, may refuse to grant this request. The problem of such a choice is entirely personal to the Sovereign, though he is, of course, free to seek informal advice from anybody whom he thinks fit to consult.
>
> Insofar as this matter can be publicly discussed, it can be properly assumed that no wise Sovereign—that is, one who has at heart the true interest of the country, the constitution, and the Monarchy—would deny a dissolution to his Prime Minister unless he were satisfied that : (1) the existing Parliament was still vital, viable, and capable of doing its job; (2) a General Election would be detrimental to the national economy; (3) he could rely on finding another Prime Minister who could carry on his Government, for a reasonable period, with a working majority in the House of Commons. . . .
>
> I am, &c,
>
> SENEX.

George VI did not face this issue in fact because Attlee's Government was not defeated and a dissolution was not requested for another eighteen months. The King's biographer reveals that George would have granted a dissolution, however, had Attlee requested it. The debate and Lascelles' interpretations of royal rights still raised a number of questions. Is the King to decide when an election is detrimental to the economy? What is "a reasonable time" for a new Prime Minister in Parliament? Should Lascelles' three conditions prevail would a Prime Minister even request a dissolution?

No monarch in recent times has had to answer these questions, and another set of circumstances paralleling those of 1950 is unlikely to confront the Crown. But the point is that dissolution does not rest entirely with the Prime Minister. And the Crown has several important reserve powers—the right to refuse a dissolution at a time of economic crisis, and the duty to find a Prime Minister when ordinary party procedures are inadequate, for example—which could be invoked in an emergency. And these reserve *powers*, while rarely used, can give real weight to the exercise of royal *influence*.[112]

The contemporary monarchy continued to play a significant if limited role in the political life of the nation, but its position in the Empire was transformed and reduced during the reign of George VI. He was Britain's last King-Emperor, surrendering the Imperial title in 1947, when India achieved its independence. In April 1949, the Conference of Commonwealth Prime Ministers devised a formula which kept India and Pakistan in the Commonwealth as "sovereign independent Republics," and allowed them to recognize the Crown as "the Head" of the Commonwealth.[113] Thereafter, monarchy could no longer claim a common allegiance, or act as the supreme symbol of imperial unity. George VI then became resident monarch of 50 million people, reigning sovereign of 156 million more overseas, and the external symbol of the Commonwealth for 400 million others.

Monarchy was first regarded as the human focus of the Empire late in Victoria's reign, at a time when the Queen was recognized as the symbol of national unity. Disraeli added imperial trappings in 1876 when the Queen was granted the title "Empress of India," an act intended to flatter Victoria and "to hide to the eyes of our own people & perhaps of the growing literary class in India the nakedness of the sword upon which we really rely."[114] The design was clear: The mystique of monarchy would stimulate loyalty for British authority. It is difficult for the historian to measure the strength of the Crown's cohesive power in the imperial context, but monarchy undoubtedly excited the affection of English-speaking peoples for Britain, and it may also have prolonged British rule in India by neutralizing to some extent political discontent in the subcontinent.[115] In the end, of course, imperial unity had to rest on common interests and ideals, and these did not exist.

Following Victoria, Edward VII fulfilled the Crown's imperial mission perfectly; he was a splendid centerpiece for Empire. He also, at the prompting of Arthur Balfour, sent the Duke of York on a goodwill tour of the Empire in 1901 in order to extend the ceremonial functions of the Crown overseas. "All the patriotic sentiment which makes such an Empire possible centres in him or centres chiefly in him," wrote Balfour, "and everything which emphasizes his personality to our kinsmen across the seas must be a gain to the Monarchy and the Empire."[116] In 1911 George became the first English monarch to visit India since Richard I when he appeared, as King-Emperor, at a magnificent durbar at Delhi. His presence, said the City Father of Bombay, "was a demonstration that the Crown was the living bond uniting many different races in different climes under the flag which stood for ideas of justice, toleration and progress."[117]

Monarchy was in the right place to reap the benefit of a further evolution of Empire marked by the Balfour Declaration of 1926 and the Statute of Westminster of 1931. The Dominions—Australia, Canada, New Zealand, South Africa, Newfoundland and Ireland—became "autonomous Communities within the British Empire" united only "by a common allegiance to the Crown." Monarchy was the "golden" and apparently indispensable link creating unity out of diversity. It was impossible to make a republic out of the Commonwealth, General Smuts had told the British Parliament in 1917, "because if you have to elect a President not only in these islands, but all over the British Empire, who will be the ruler and representative of all these peoples, you are facing an absolutely insoluble problem."[118] Even those who rejected the idea of royal mystique admitted the Crown was no longer an anachronism; there were "insuperable difficulties in providing for an elective headship"[119] for the Commonwealth.

Royalists tried to invest the Crown link with special magical powers, but it is difficult to take seriously Robert Menzies' contention that the "notion of the Crown and a common allegiance ran through" the first Commonwealth "like a rod of steel,"[120] or Churchill's rhetoric of the Crown as a "mysterious link, indeed, I may say the magic link" binding Empire.[121] The cohesive powers of monarchy were insufficient to overcome inner tensions which increasingly weakened bonds of union within the Commonwealth. But in 1956 Menzies spoke of a "Crown Commonwealth" within the total Commonwealth, and maintained that the Crown was still an essential ingredient in government and national life in the old Dominions.[122] Even this statement needs qualification. There was no common allegiance in the Commonwealth, P.C. Gordon Walker wrote in 1953: "It is not common in the sense that it is everywhere of the same substance or that it everywhere expresses itself in the same forms. It is rather a set of distinct but parallel allegiances."[123]

Today the Crown is still the head of state for external and internal purposes in Canada, Australia and New Zealand, but the Irish Free State became a Republic and left the Commonwealth in 1949, as South Africa did in 1961. In Canada high feeling for monarchy does not exist in French-speaking areas, so that it has become a possible hindrance to unity. Prime Minister Pierre Trudeau hinted at the future when he said in December 1969: "I think there will be a great deal of change in the 1970s. . . . The values of the new generation and tremendous technological changes may lead Canada to give up its connections with the royal family in the coming decade."[124] In Australia a Gallup poll in the summer of 1970 found 68 per cent of Australians would prefer Prince Charles as King after his mother's reign. But 26 per cent sought a republic, and 6 per cent were undecided.[125] It is possible to see the movement away from monarchial forms in the Empire, begun under George VI, ending with only New Zealand and a few islands as part of the "Crown Commonwealth." Because of the trend of political nationalism, an ardent monarchist in Britain concludes, "It is safest to think of the future of monarchy in the context only of the British Isles."[126]

George VI was saddened by the changes taking place within the Empire during his reign, but they were beyond his control, and he had no more thought of resisting them than he had of impeding social-political movements at home. A more dynamic and ambitious man might have prevented a smooth adjustment to these fundamental alterations. As it was, the Crown served to legitimize them, and to cushion the psychological blow many in Britain experienced with the loss of the old Empire.

The King left his inheritance in the safe hands of his daughter. Elizabeth II admired her father, and fits easily into his conception of monarchy. She has his shyness, but also his sense of duty; "She is a planner, a hard worker, sometimes a worrier. She has a very high concept of the duties of queenship."[127] The Queen is devoted to her family, and to those country relaxations enjoyed by her grandfather: riding, shooting and deerstalking. Royal holidays are spent in the traditional retreats, Windsor, Sandringham and Balmoral.

Elizabeth II carries out her business duties conscientiously and methodically; she reads state papers carefully, and is an exceedingly well-informed person. Yet the powers of the Crown have declined during her reign. In 1965 the Conservatives adopted an elective system of leadership similar to Labour's, which in practice takes the appointment of a Prime Minister out of the monarch's hands.[128] Before 1965 the death or retirement of a Conservative Prime Minister meant that the monarch was sometimes involved in party struggles over the choice of a new Premier who became, in effect, the leader of the party as well. This was the case when the Crown was caught up in a certain amount of controversy over the selection of Harold Macmillan to replace Anthony Eden in 1957 and Sir Alec Douglas-Home to replace Macmillan in 1963. Under the new selective process the Crown has less responsibility, but at the same time less power. Another sign of the waning power of the Crown came in 1967 when the Labour Government introduced a plan to abolish the hereditary basis of the House of Lords.[129] Pressures within the House of Commons forced the Government to withdraw the reform measures, but the Palace accepted them in principle, even though they would eliminate another of those flying buttresses of hereditary monarchy.

The Queen still expresses her views, however, and because of her position can expect to be listened to with respect. The outlook of the Palace is not taken lightly, as Drew Middleton recently observed:

> Early in 1956 I was talking to an important civil servant about a government decision that was to be announced in the next few days. The government was busy making certain, he said, that "the Palace" wouldn't "make a row about it." I said I was surprised that he should ascribe so much weight to the Palace's view in a matter that involved the Cabinet and the House of Commons. His answer was that in a country such as Britain under a Conservative government influence is not exerted solely through the House or government departments. "What people say to each other counts," he said. "And when the Queen says it, it counts a great deal. Of course, she couldn't change a decision. Nor would she attempt to. But it can be awkward, you know."[130]

Elizabeth II is already a formidable woman, and should she exercise her rights wisely, she could become a formidable influence in Government as she grows older. According to the *New Statesman*:

> A British monarch's theoretical powers do not increase with the duration of the reign—on the contrary—but the personality becomes much more difficult to handle. The Queen already possesses more public experience than most of her ministers. The time will come when her premiers are her juniors in age, too, and vastly her juniors in service. Her health is excellent. She may well still be on the throne at the end of the century, advised by men now at school. The example of Queen Victoria, whom she resembles in more ways than one, suggests that they will be made to earn their emoluments.[131]

Only a popular monarch could command such attention, and Elizabeth II has the respect of the country because she is solidifying the synthesis of kingship created by George V, briefly interrupted by Edward VIII, and revived by George VI.

---

[1] Quoted in Keith Middlemas and John Barnes, *Baldwin*, p. 976.

[2] A.G. Gardiner, *Portraits and Portents*, p. 75.

[3] The *Times*, January 22, 1936.

[4] See Duke of Windsor, *A King's Story*, p. 338, and Lewis Broad, *The Abdication*, p. 81.

[5] A large number of these incidents are recounted in W. and L. Townsend, *The Biography of H. R. H. The Prince of Wales*.

[6] Duke of Windsor, *A King's Story*, p. 282.

[7] *Ibid.*, p. 287.

[8] *Ibid.*, p. 134.

[9] *Ibid.*

[10] James Pope-Hennessy, *Queen Mary*, p. 445.

[11] Duke of Windsor, *A King's Story*, p. 104.

[12] Duchess of Windsor, *The Heart Has Its Reasons*, p. 222. During his summer vacation aboard the *Nahlin*, Edward stood on the bridge dressed only in shorts when the yacht, watched by the Greeks, passed through the Corinth Canal. Helen Hardinge, *Loyal To Three Kings*, p. 108, gives another example of Edward's lack of dignity on some occasions. While in Vienna he wandered around naked in the steam-room of a public bath house.

[13] Duke of Windsor, *A King's Story*, p. 132, and James Pope-Hennessy, *Queen Mary*, p. 446.

[14] Duke of Windsor, *A King's Story*, p. 194.

[15] Thomas Jones, *A Diary With Letters, 1931–1950*, p. 291.

[16] Duke of Windsor, *A King's Story*, p. 276.

[17] Duchess of Windsor, *The Heart Has Its Reasons*, p. 215.

[18] Walter Bagehot, *The English Constitution*, p. 40.

[19] Duke of Windsor, *A King's Story*, p. 138.

[20] J. G. Lockhard, *Cosmo Gordon Lang*, p. 395.

[21] Keith Middlemas and John Barnes, *Baldwin*, p. 978.

[22] Iain MacLeod, *Neville Chamberlain*, p. 198.

[23] Robert Rhodes James, ed., *Memoirs of a Conservative*, p. 19.

[24] Dennis Bardens, *Portrait of a Statesman*, p. 146.

[25] Duke of Windsor, *A King's Story*, p. 256.

[26] Robert Rhodes James, ed., *Memoirs of a Conservative*, p. 178.

[27] Duke of Windsor, *A King's Story*, p. 132.

[28] Keith Middlemas and John Barnes, *Baldwin*, p. 979.

[29] See Helen Hardinge, *Loyal To Three Kings*, pp. 83–84, 89–90 for a critical discussion of Edward's work habits.

[30] Duke of Windsor, *A King's Story*, p. 28.

[31] Keith Middlemas and John Barnes, *Baldwin*, p. 979.

[32] Aneurin Bevan, the flamboyant Socialist M.P. from South Wales, refused to accompany Edward on his tour of South Wales because royalty was used to mask persecution, to supply "a fertile source of political diversion," and to keep society as it was. See Michael Foot, *Aneurin Bevan*, I, 239–41.

[33] Duke of Windsor, *A King's Story*, p. 279.

[34] Lewis Broad, *The Abdication*, p. 82.

35 Robert Graves and Alan Hodge, *The Long Week End*, pp. 308–09.
36 Herbert Morrison, *Government and Parliament*, p. 82.
37 Dennis Bardens, *Portrait of a Statesman*, p. 145.
38 Duke of Windsor, *A King's Story*, pp. 279, 298–99.
39 Quoted in Brian Inglis, *Abdication*, pp. 70–71.
40 Keith Middlemas and John Barnes, *Baldwin*, p. 979.
41 *Ibid.,* p. 980.
42 Hugh Dalton, *The Fateful Years, 1931–1945*, p. 112.
43 Jessica Mitford, *Hons and Rebels*, p. 93.
44 A.J.P. Taylor, *English History, 1914–1945*, p. 489.
45 For example, Warre Bradley's *Why Edward Went*.
46 Lord Beaverbrook, *The Abdication Of King Edward VIII*, p. 13.
47 Keith Middlemas and John Barnes, *Baldwin*, p. 995.
48 Lewis Broad, *The Abdication*, pp. 23–24.
49 C.V. Wedgwood, *Our Queen, Crown and Monarchy*, pp. 6–7.
50 Duchess of Windsor, *The Heart Has Its Reasons*, p. 181.
51 Lord Beaverbrook, *The Abdication Of King Edward VIII*, p. 14. It was known, says Helen Hardinge, as "Ritz Bar society." (*Loyal To Three Kings*, p. 73.)
52 Duchess of Windsor, *The Heart Has Its Reasons*, p. 192.
53 Duke of Windsor, *A King's Story*, p. 258.
54 *Ibid.,* p. 276.
55 John Evelyn Wrench, *Geoffrey Dawson and Our Times*, p. 337.
56 Duchess of Windsor, *The Heart Has Its Reasons*, p. 219.
57 Cecil Beaton, *Photobiography*, p. 88.
58 Duchess of Windsor, *The Heart Has Its Reasons*, p. 219.
59 Keith Middlemas and John Barnes, *Baldwin*, p. 981.
60 *Ibid.,* pp. 981–85.
61 *Ibid.*
62 Humphrey Jennings, et. al., *May The Twelfth*, p. 302.
63 G.M. Young, *Stanley Baldwin*, pp. 238–39. Lord Beaverbrook, *The Abdication of King Edward VIII*, p. 60, charges that Baldwin framed the question to the Dominions in blunt and uncompromising terms. But in fact the telegrams were prepared by the Dominions Office. See Keith Middlemas and John Barnes, *Baldwin*, p. 976, and Lord Birkenhead, *Walter Monckton*, pp. 140, 159. Edward himself suggested consulting Dominion Governments, apparently expecting his great popularity would persuade them to give approval.
64 The *Times*, December 8, 1936.
65 Thomas Jones, *A Diary With Letters, 1931–1950*, p. 296.
66 See Lewis Broad, *The Abdication*, pp. 79–80.
67 Duke of Windsor, *A King's Story*, p. 361.
68 Hardinge's letter is reproduced in John Wheeler-Bennett, *King George VI*, p. 280.
69 Robert Rhodes James, ed., *Chips: The Diaries of Sir Henry Channon*, p. 78.
70 Nicolson, Harold, *Diaries And Letters*, I, 281–82.
71 Keith Middlemas and John Barnes, *Baldwin*, pp. 988–89.
72 Robert Rhodes James, ed., *Memoirs of a Conservative*, p. 416.
73 Keith Middlemas and John Barnes, *Baldwin*, pp. 988–89.
74 James Pope-Hennessy, *Queen Mary*, p. 575.
75 Keith Middlemas and John Barnes, *Baldwin*, p. 1006.
76 *Ibid.,* pp. 1008–09.
77 Lord Beaverbrook, *The Abdication Of King Edward VIII*, pp. 51, 52, 54.
78 *Ibid.,* pp. 58–59.
79 Sir Charles Petrie, *The Modern British Monarchy*, p. 174.
80 Hugh Dalton, *The Fateful Years, 1931–1945*, pp. 113–14.
81 Colin Cross, *The Fascists In Britain*, pp. 164–65. The Communist Party also pledged support of Edward. Harry Pollitt, the Communist leader, maintained: "There is no crisis in all this business for the working class. Let the King marry whom he likes. That is his personal business." See Robert Graves and Alan Hodge, *The Long Week End*, p. 353.
82 Hugh Dalton, *The Fateful Years, 1931–1945*, p. 113–14.
83 Brian Inglis, *Abdication*, p. 347.
84 Lord Beaverbrook, *The Abdication Of King Edward VIII*, p. 80.
85 Duke of Windsor, *A King's Story*, p. 413.
86 For example, Winston Churchill and Colonel Josiah C. Wedgwood. See Lord Beaverbrook, *The Abdication Of King Edward VIII*, p. 109, and Josiah C. Wedgwood, *Memoirs Of A Fighting Life*, p.235.
87 L. S. Amery, *My Political Life*, III, 217.
88 J. G. Lockhard, *Cosmo Gordon Lang*, p. 405.
89 Lord Birkenhead, *Walter Monckton*, p. 128, and Duke of Windsor, *A King's Story*, p. 280.
90 Quoted in Lord Birkenhead, *Walter Monckton*, p. 158.

[91] Robert Rhodes James, ed., *Chips: The Diaries of Sir Henry Channon*, p. 97.

[92] The phrase of Churchill. See Keith Middlemas and John Barnes, *Baldwin*, p. 1016.

[93] For a summary of newspaper opinion see *The New Statesman And Nation*, December 5, 1936.

[94] J. G. Lockhard, *Cosmo Gordon Lang*, p. 404.

[95] Lord Beaverbrook, *The Abdication Of King Edward VIII*, pp. 110–14.

[96] Dermot Morrah, "The Social Monarchy," p. 172, in Jeremy Murray-Brown, ed., *The Monarchy and Its Future*. This is, in fact, the core of the problem of the monarchy's adaptation to modern society. As W.H. Auden notes in "The Queen Is Never Bored," (*New Yorker*, May 21, 1960, p. 165): "It is probable . . . that the more permissive society becomes about manners and morals, the stricter will be the demands it makes upon its Sacred Beings. The sovereign is always one for whom an exception is made. In the past, there was an exception of license; the King could openly keep mistresses, while his subjects could commit adultery only in secret. In the future, it would seem that the sovereign must be an exception whose fidelity in marriage is notorious; in a licentious democracy a King Farouk is impossible."

[97] J. G. Lockhard, *Cosmo Gordon Lang*, p. 407.

[98] Duke of Windsor, *A King's Story*, p. 260.

[99] Christopher Hibbert, *The Court at Windsor*, p. 281. ·

[100] Robert Rhodes James, ed., *Chips: The Diaries of Sir Henry Channon*, p. 119.

[101] *Ibid.*, p. 463.

[102] Harold Nicolson, *Diaries and Letters*, II, 462.

[103] The analysis above is based on C.V. Wedgwood's description of royal portraits. See her *Our Queen, Crown and Monarchy*, p. 11.

[104] John W. Wheeler-Bennett, *King George VI*, p. 151.

[105] *Ibid.*, p. 293.

[106] John Winant, *A Letter from Grosvenor Square*, pp. 19–20.

[107] Robert Rhodes James, ed., *Memoirs of a Conservative*, p. 177.

[108] On this matter see John W. Wheeler-Bennett, *King George VI*, pp. 431–34; Iain MacLeod, *Neville Chamberlain*, pp. 284–87; Robert Rhodes James, ed., *Chips: The Diaries of Sir Henry Channon*, pp. 228–29; R. J. Minney, *The Private Papers of Hore-Belisha*, pp. 257–78.

[109] See John W. Wheeler-Bennett, *King George VI*, pp. 637–39; Francis Williams, *A Prime Minister Remembers*, p. 5; Alan Bullock, *The Life and Times of Ernest Bevin*, II, 393–95.

[110] John W. Wheeler-Bennett, *King George VI*, pp. 661–65.

[111] The *Times*, May 2, 1950.

[112] See John W. Wheeler-Bennett, *King George VI*, pp. 771–75 and Robert Blake's essay "The Crown and Politics in the Twentieth Century," in Jeremy Murray-Brown, ed., *The Monarchy and Its Future*.

[113] N. Mansergh, ed., *Documents and Speeches on British Commonwealth Affairs*, 1931–1952, pp. 846–47.

[114] Robert Blake, *Disraeli*, pp. 562–63.

[115] See, for example, the essay "The Jewel In the Crown" by the Indian novelist Sasthi Brata in Jeremy Murray-Brown, ed., *The Monarchy and Its Future*.

[116] Harold Nicolson, *King George V*, p. 67.

[117] Jeremy Murray-Brown, ed., *The Monarchy and Its Future*, p. 31.

[118] W. K. Hancock and Jean Van Der Poel, eds., *Selections From the Smuts Papers*, III, 513.

[119] Sidney and Beatrice Webb, *A Constitution For The Socialist Commonwealth of Great Britain*, p. 109.

[120] The *Times*, June 11 and 12, 1956.

[121] Frank Underhill, *The British Commonwealth*, p. 82.

[122] The *Times*, June 11 and 12, 1956.

[123] P.C. Gordon Walker, "Crown Divisible," *The Twentieth Century*, June 1953, pp. 425–29.

[124] Quoted in Andrew Duncan, *The Reality of Monarchy*, p. 65.

[125] *The Guardian*, July 24, 1970.

[126] The statement of Dermot Morrah, found in Jeremy Murray-Brown, ed., *The Monarchy and Its Future*, p. 175.

[127] Dorothy Laird, *How The Queen Reigns*, p. 36. On Elizabeth II and her court see Laird and Andrew Duncan, *The Reality of Monarchy*.

[128] The system is outlined briefly in R.M. Punnett, *British Government and Politics*, pp. 112–13.

[129] See *Ibid.*, pp. 264–69.

[130] Drew Middleton, *These Are The British*, pp. 21–22.

[131] *New Statesman*, August 23, 1968.

CHAPTER 5

THE MONARCHY AND ITS FUTURE

In this age of opinion polls and social surveys the royal family must submit to a type of public review from time to time. It is impossible to say whether the Palace pays any attention to these popular assessments but they do produce interesting statistics on current attitudes on royalty.

A recent sociological survey may offer an index of the future. In 1969 a team of sociologists interviewed a cross-section of 12-year-old children in England in order to test their notions of monarchy. Most of the children viewed the Queen as a symbol of benevolence and helpfulness, an outlook, it is said, many will carry into adolescence and even adulthood. Three-fifths of those interviewed thought the Queen was the most important person in England; less than one-half named the Prime Minister. The children also believed that the country should turn to the Queen when critical decisions were faced.[1]

In the sixties Mass-Observation made two surveys in order to assess adult views on royalty. Their samples, broken down by sex, age groups and socio-economic status, give the results shown in Table 1.[2]

In its interviews Mass-Observation asked people why they valued monarchy; their answers strongly endorsed the main features of the Georgian synthesis. The institution was expected to fulfill four purposes: (1) Provide a basis for political stability by denying reverence but not power to the politicians; (2) Give a focus of personal interest and affection, which is a source of psychological security; (3) Set an example to the nation in personal and family life, and public service; (4) Provide pageantry and ceremonial, which brings glamor, mystery and excitement. The last of the four, it was implied, enhanced the effectiveness of others.[3]

Intellectuals, for their part, engaged in a wide-ranging debate on the "Condition of Britain" in the sixties and subjected almost every institution in the country to a searching criticism. Monarchy emerged from the review far better than the efficient parts of the constitution—Commons and Cabinet—but attention was once again focused on those twin problems of cost and style. The Duke of Edinburgh brought these issues

Table 1. ASSESSMENT OF ROYALTY

	ENTIRELY FAVORABLE %	LARGELY FAVORABLE %	MIXED FEELINGS %	LARGELY UNFAVORABLE %	ENTIRELY UNFAVORABLE %	DON'T KNOW AND UNINTERESTED %
Total Poll	60	9	7	3	10	11
Men	53	8	8	3	15	13
Women	67	9	6	3	6	9
16–24	54	8	5	5	16	12
25–44	53	10	9	5	11	11
45–64	64	9	7	2	8	10
Over 65	73	6	5	1	7	8
Upper and Middle Class	67	12	6	3	4	8
Lower Middle Class	69	10	10	4	6	11
Skilled Working Class	58	10	5	4	11	12
Unskilled Working Class	60	6	9	2	13	10

dramatically before the country when he appeared on Meet the Press in the United States on November 9, 1969, and announced, somewhat tactlessly, that the Palace would "go into the red" in 1970 and might have to move into smaller premises.[4] Following this comment, the Prime Minister, after prior consultation with political leaders and the Court, announced that a select committee of the House would review the Queen's income from the Civil List in 1970. The committee was actually appointed in 1971. Its report, and the ensuing debate in the Commons, will undoubtedly lift the curtain on much of the mystery that surrounds royal finance and will probably determine the scale of grandeur and ceremony at which the British monarchy will operate in the future.

A lively public disputation, which would have been considered impertinent early in the century, followed the Duke's television performance. Many of those of leftist political persuasion refused to shed tears over the financial plight of the Palace, arguing that charity should not begin with monarchy. They preferred a less expensive one anyway, modeled after those in Scandinavia, the so-called bicycle monarchies. The Crown was no longer the cynosure of a world empire, said the *New Statesman*, and so its expensive trappings were no more relevant in 1969 than British gunboats east of Suez. It was absurd to have the Imperial Crown "blaze away in a vacuum." The British people had also learned to conduct themselves in more modest fashion than in Victorian times and so it made simple moral sense to shut down a palace or two.[5] Even those who wish to retain a splendid monarchy are urging the Palace to open up its books; a careful scrutiny by Parliament might take royal finance out of public controversy. They are convinced the British people are willing to pay the price for royal splendor, for only this can symbolize the country's historic past, and allow monarchy to fulfill its functions of the present. Only a certain style, says the *Spectator*, can create "the conditions of majesty and mystery necessary to enable an ordinary family to command the public awe and respect which a head of state must command if he or she is to become a genuine focus of national unity and symbol of the nation itself."[6] Of course Parliament—and eventually the public itself—will set the level of royal expenditure and style. Britons do not seem to expect their monarchy to live in humble surroundings, and so it will probably continue to be the "Rolls Royce" of monarchies.

The actual cost of monarchy is unknown, which is why estimates vary so widely, ranging from £2 million to over £7 million annually. A recent source has calculated the total annual cost to the public as follows:

	£	$
Civil List	475,000	1,140,000
Consolidated fund (mostly for salaries of other royal personages)	160,000	384,000
Palaces	1,056,431	2,535,434
Britannia (royal yacht)	500,000	1,200,000
Royal flight	450,000	1,080,000
Telephone bill	51,000	122,000
Postage	6,000	14,000
Total	2,698,431	6,476,234

The main item in dispute is the Civil List, which was fixed by Parliament in 1952. This is the Queen's personal housekeeping budget out of which she pays the expenses and salaries of a royal household of around 300. A small amount, the Royal Bounty, is for charities. A supplementary provision of £95,000 a year was added in 1952 as a cushion against inflation but this allowance of 20 per cent proved insufficient because of the Queen's long reign. It is the Civil List which began to run in the red in 1970.[8]

The sovereign's private income and fortune are enormous, so that the Queen is able to supplement the Civil List out of private funds until it is revised. The income comes principally from the lands and investments of the Duchy of Lancaster, which pay the Queen over £200,000 yearly. Prince Charles is entitled to the income of the Duchy of Cornwall, also over £200,000 a year, but he turns one half of this over to the Treasury. The Queen's private fortune is estimated at between £50 million and £60 million. This includes her houses at Sandringham and Balmoral, her investments, the royal farms, and the royal collection of jewels, art, silver, porcelain and stamps. Estate taxes, which decimate most great fortunes in the country, are not paid by the Queen, and little is known about other taxes levied on royal income, investments and property. The suspicion and speculation frequently attached to royal expenditures and income can only harm the prestige of monarchy; perhaps the select committee of 1970 will dig deeper and make more disclosures about royal finance than committees have done in the past, and this may finally end much of the mystery, muddle and controversy.

Apart from alleged extravagance the charge most often levelled against the Crown is that it is failing to meet "the challenge of change." Critics urge the monarchy to "move with the times," develop a "contemporary image," be more "with it," exhibit more "adaptability to changing realities," and become more "relevant." And the slowness to adapt is most evident, they claim, with the Queen's entourage, which is a tight little enclave of British "ladies and gentlemen," and the royal manner, which is too formal and pompous.[9]

Most of the Queen's household and friends are indeed drawn from the territorial aristocracy. Courtiers are usually old Etonians, and ex-guards officers, and the ladies are duchesses or countesses, or their daughters. They are, writes a Labour Member of Parliament, William Hamilton, "a strange baggage with which to march fearlessly towards the white heat of the late-twentieth century of technological and scientific revolution."[10] The Court has made little response to these criticisms because the Queen, like her father and grandfather, dislikes changes in personnel. She inherited many of her courtiers from her father's court; replacements are made only because of death or retirement. In 1967, however, a young Australian was named as the Queen's Press Secretary, and this appointment may be a signal of others to come.

However, the Court is becoming more accessible to "ordinary" subjects. In 1956, for example, the Queen began giving informal luncheons at the Palace for "interesting personalities from every kind of life." She had 1700 guests between 1956 and 1969. Large afternoon garden parties are also staged twice a year at Buckingham Palace so that she may honor thousands of people "prominent in all forms of society." Presentation parties for debutantes were abolished in 1957.[11] These changes are not radical enough to satisfy the critics, but they reflect a gradual modernization of the Court.

Less formality and antique ritual would also enhance the survival powers of monarchy, say the modernizers. The Queen should come out from behind deadening protocol, lift the curtain on mystery, and appear as a warm, relaxed and ordinary person. As a concession to these pressures a film about the royal family gave millions a glimpse into the intimate private lives of the royals in 1969. The response to the film was not entirely favorable, however. Some prefer the symbol of majesty, and fear that an overemphasis upon the homey and the human will cheapen the Crown. According to the *Sunday Telegraph*:

> Now that we have seen the Queen buying lollipops for Prince Edward, or helping prepare a family barbeque in the grounds of Balmoral Castle, will the next solemn process of the Garter Knights at Windsor, with her Majesty at the Head, seem more dignified, or more ludicrous? The Greek gods came down to earth for a while as men, and their worshippers seemed to like them all the better for it. But can the same be said for mere constitutional monarchs who then proceed to turn themselves into mere mortals?
>
> One has a feeling that it is precisely they who have most to risk from too much bridging of the gap. The monarchy has a safe niche as the romantic personification of what Britain was. It is more doubtful how it can be made as yet to personify what Britain is—particularly as the nation seems very unclear on this point itself.[12]

Responding to popular pressures is a tricky business for monarchy. On occasion and especially in times of crisis, a heightened magnificence is required; but often the country appears to wish a kind of "idealized ordinariness." The continued popularity of monarchy suggests that the royals are doing rather well—at least to date—in finding the right balance.[13]

The popularity of the modern British monarchy reflects a successful interaction between royal behavior and popular demand. The right response on the part of the Crown in the past century has frequently been accidental, of course, but it also involved some political wisdom. This was often applied by the sovereign's private secretary, who will undoubtedly continue to play a key role in maintaining good relations between the Crown and its subjects.

The office was first held in its modern form by Sir Henry Ponsonby, who was appointed by Queen Victoria in 1870. Since then only seven men have held the post, and the present holder, Sir Michael Adeane, is the grandson of Sir Arthur Bigge, later Lord Stamfordham, who was private secretary to Queen Victoria and George V. The office is obviously an extremely important one, in fact Lord Rosebery called it "the most important in the public service."[14] The private secretary acts, it is sometimes said, as the monarch's "personal Prime Minister," and John Wheeler-Bennett suggests that his pattern of conduct epitomizes the formula of the royal prerogative; he must advise, encourage, and warn the monarch as to the courses he should pursue. The monarch depends upon him for information on all affairs. He checks all incoming boxes, bringing to the sovereign's notice all important documents, and summarizing those of less importance. He draws upon many sources of information, including government ministers, opposition leaders, back-benchers in Parliament, senior civil servants, churchmen, lawyers, elder statesmen, union leaders and captains of industry. All communications between Governor-Generals and the Palace pass through his hands.

Harold Laski's comments on the role of the private secretary are most illuminating:

> The royal secretary walks on a tight-rope below which he is never unaware that an abyss is yawning. If the Monarch is lazy, like Edward VII, his very presence may almost become an error of judgment. If the Monarch is hardworking, like Queen Victoria, all his tact and discretion are required to keep firmly drawn the possible lines of working relations in a constitutional system. He has to be himself, since his sincerity is the crux of his position; but he must never be so insistently himself that Ministers are disturbed by his influence. It is vital that he be a judge of character; he has to thread his way through a host of influences the effective measurement of which is essential to the Monarch's position. He has to translate the obvious decisions of common sense into the elaborate formulae which the etiquette of the system requires. He must accept its pomps and ceremonies without fatigue; and he must be able to make the elegant minuet he is constantly performing capable of adaptation to a world which is constantly changing. Half of him must be in a real sense a statesman, and the other half must be prepared, if the occasion arise, to be something it is not very easy to distinguish from a lacquey. . . .
>
> For he has to put aside personal views; a private secretary to the Monarch who pushed his ideas might easily precipitate a crisis. He must be pretty nearly selfless; once private ambition begins to colour his horizons, his usefulness is over. He must move serenely amid all the events which move other men to passionate statement; he must seem, therefore, never to feel while he never appears to be without the power of sympathetic response. The secretary to the Monarch, in short, occupies to the Crown much the same position that the Crown itself in our system occupies to the Government; he must advise and encourage and warn. But whereas the Monarch can speak his mind—as we know from the royal letters of the last hundred years—the private secretary has no such luxury. He interprets as best he can a tradition which is never quite the same from one Monarch

to another with the same Monarch. . . .

. . . I do not think it is beyond the mark to say that a bad private secretary, one who was rash, or indiscreet, or untrustworthy, might easily make the system of constitutional monarchy unworkable unless the Monarch himself was a person of extraordinary wisdom. This is so because the system is built on compromises, accommodations, a process of half-measures, in which an attempt, on either side, to dominate might rapidly produce an explosive atmosphere. The Monarch, with us, has grown in influence as he has surrendered power and the very fact of that growth means that those who are playing for power will seek to capture his influence. To keep the Monarch nicely balanced in the delicate position he occupies is likely to call for a diplomatic talent of the first order.[15]

Private secretaries operate behind the scenes, and so it is not often that the historian can assign to them definite influence on events. An exception is Lord Knollys' decisive advice in the constitutional crisis of 1910; it is possible, too, that Lord Stamfordham played a key role in the appointment of Baldwin as Prime Minister in 1923. Their greatest achievement, however, has been the successful response monarchy has made to social change in the country since Victoria's day.

Some modern critics have suggested that the private secretary should be appointed by the Prime Minister, or by a Civil Service Commission, but he is still named solely at the discretion of the Crown. Sovereigns have shown exceptionally good judgment in the selection of their private secretaries, and as long as this record is maintained pressures to have their appointment taken out of the hands of the Crown are not likely to mount.

It is clear, however, that the problems facing the monarchy are exceedingly delicate, and will require the greatest possible tact, on the part of the royal family itself and on the part of its closest advisers. One problem, for example, is the question of education: Ought the young princes and princesses to attend state schools, and thus mingle with "ordinary" people in order to prepare them better to symbolize the nation as a whole? Or, on the other hand, would such an education be affected and condescending? After all, the Prince of Wales is not just another boy; as Prince Charles is alleged to have said, how can I be treated like everyone else when my mother's picture is on all the money? The Queen and Prince Philip thus far have tried to strike a happy medium. They sent Prince Charles to Gordonstoun which, although hardly a state school for the "ordinary" child, does not have the "elitist" aura of an Eton, Harrow, or Winchester. Furthermore, the Prince was then sent to a school in Australia, and great publicity was devoted to its ruggedness and openness. The problem, as indicated above, is basically one of balancing majesty and mystery with characteristics with which the mass of the people are able to identify, all the while avoiding ridiculousness.

Should the monarch ever become an entirely empty symbol it will be ridiculous. The allegation of emptiness was at the heart of the strong attack leveled at the throne by John Osborne in the 1950s. Osborne claimed that royalty was "the gold filling in a mouthful of decay," because it shielded men from an appreciation of reality; as one historian has summed up Osborne's view, "while people can see the gloved hand waving from the golden coach, they feel assured that all is well with the nation, whatever its true state."[16] Yet even the angriest of the angry young men of the 1950s seem to be turning away from their once strongly held views, and are moving toward what may be a broader and more realistic appreciation of society; one may wonder if this does not indicate that the allegation of the monarchy's superficiality is not superficial itself, for society is something far more subtle than an analysis limited to political, social and economic problems might indicate.

A nation benefits from a symbol or a representative who, although not necessarily divorced from politics, is beyond politics. Such a symbol is extremely useful in handing out honors, for example, for a decoration or a title, although its origin may clearly be political, comes formally from the nation as a whole, and not from the immediate recipient of the services rendered. As a result it means more. J.B. Priestly probably had this in mind when he wrote:

> Somebody has to hand out medals, lay foundation stones, and receive the Boojum of Banana. In America the President is saddled with all this, while he is trying to run his own vast country and a good slice of ours. Why not then employ some smiling and experienced professionals who, existing as they do in a mysterious golden haze, are far more glamorous figures than successful party politicians? There are of course some countries in which the president is not a politician but some bumbling old figurehead. But whose heart would beat faster because he was about to receive a medal from President Betjeman?[17]

It is also worth remembering that a monarch may act as a brake on the awarding of unwarranted honors, as George V tried to do, although with limited success, with Lloyd George. Furthermore, the heightened value of an honor that comes from the sovereign has been increasingly appreciated in this century. One of Edward VII's most notable innovations was the establishment of the Order of Merit, Britain's most prestigious decoration, which is entirely in the gift of the Crown. And the Attlee Government returned the Order of the Garter, England's and Europe's leading order of chivalry, to the gift of the sovereign shortly after the Second World War.[18]

The twentieth century has brought to the forefront one of the most valuable attributes of the monarchy, which has been briefly touched on in earlier chapters. The Crown lowers the prestige, and the psychological leverage, of politicians. A totalitarian dictator, for example, must use his po-

litical power for more than political purposes; he must use it as a spring-
board to achieve dominance in all areas of the nation's and the individual's
life. Yet the Crown provides an alternative focus of loyalty which can
shortcircuit such ambitions, by denying politicians the reverence and the
psychological power which being head of state as well as head of government can give them. Winston Churchill may well have been correct when
he suggested that the survival of the Hohenzollern dynasty in Germany
after the First World War might have blocked Hitler's rise to power.[19] A
German emperor might have been more effective in stopping the Nazis
than an aged field marshal who symbolized a regime he himself disliked. A
better example is Italy, where the House of Savoy, although it could not
block Mussolini's political domination, did act as a barrier to the Duce's totalitarian ambitions; Victor Emmanuel III was always there to remind
Mussolini of the survival of traditional values, and those who disliked the
Fascist regime could cling to their loyalty to the throne. Hitler, for one,
could never understand why Mussolini tolerated the monarchy, and was
infuriated during his state visit to Italy in 1938 when protocol demanded
that he be received by the King, ride through the streets in a royal coach,
and stay for several days at the Palace, where he was snubbed by the
Court. Hitler realized that the monarchy, simply by existing, was blocking
the fulfillment of the Fascist revolution.[20]

Perhaps yet another example of the influence of monarchy can be seen
in the Second World War, when the King of Italy and the Emperor of
Japan were able to enforce a policy which got their countries out of the
war:

> . . . a critical difference between wartime Germany on the one hand
> and Italy and Japan on the other was that the latter two countries,
> though quasi-totalitarian, had in their monarchial systems a latent
> means of crystallizing an effective and legal opposition to the war
> party.[21]

A monarchy can do a great deal, moreover, in a democratic or liberal nation like Britain, by removing the nation itself from the middle of controversy. The fury and the anger of political battle will, often if not always,
be focused more sharply on the issues themselves if a principal figure in
the controversy is not also the supreme representative of the nation. It is
hard to differentiate, for example, between the President of the United
States as the symbol of the country, and the President as a political leader.
In times of tension and turmoil the nation cannot help but be weakened
by the inevitable attacks on its leader; nor, on the other hand, is the cause
of political freedom and open discussion helped by the equally inevitable
tendency of the President to shield himself from criticism by wrapping
himself in the flag and claiming that any criticism of him is unpatriotic. A
monarchy is not by any means a complete protection against such tactics
on the part of a politician but, with the ultimate position in the state

beyond his reach and in the hands of a person who embodies the entire history of the nation, who has never been directly involved in politics, and who is beyond the reach of political ambition, the temptation and possibility are greatly reduced.

None of this means, of course, that the monarchy can be justified only on the basis of what it prevents. The Queen performs many formal and necessary functions with great ability and charm, and also plays an important political role by being a neutral, but an experienced, informed, and tough-minded center of the parliamentary system. As has been discussed above, as her reign lengthens, so does her knowledge, which, if brought to bear with tact and common-sense, can have a subtle but important influence in the nation's life. No Prime Minister need take her advice, but her prestige and position demand that attention be paid to her suggestions and questions; policies will be none the worse for being rethought at the Queen's request, and, since the request is always private, no one's pride can suffer if the royal request results in a modification of policy.

One cannot tell if the monarchy has a future, but it has been extremely adaptable in the past, and, in an age of mass-production, mass-communication, and mass-alienation, it has shown itself able to play a vital role in personalizing the state and all the complexities of modern government. As Bagehot realized, the activities of individuals are always more interesting than the impersonal functions of a bureaucracy. If the monarchy tends to make one think in a way which is more oriented toward tradition, continuity, and stability than toward change, dynamism, and tension, it need not blind one to the necessity of responding effectively to changing conditions. One can argue just as effectively that, by providing a degree of certainty and familiarity, it can open the way to social change that is all the more effective because it is legitimized by being announced in a traditional manner and carried out by traditional means. A part of everyone's personality demands security; if the monarchy provides that security, the other part of the personality may be more willing to change. The reforms of the post-war Labour Government probably seemed at least a little less frightening to many Britons because, after all, they were announced by the King, surrounded by his Court, from the throne in the House of Lords.

Of course, the monarchy will always inspire hostility in those who wish to see a complete revolution in the nation's life; they will see the Crown as an institution which blinds one to reality, perpetuates snobbery, and forces a reactionary frame of mind on the nation. But such people should come to understand, as have many other republicans in the past, that both history and psychology indicate that a nation is more complex than their over-rationalizations allow; they might also remember that revolutions which start with a highly idealized desire to achieve the millenium, or a reasonable facsimile thereof, often end with a Cromwell, a Robespierre, a Napoleon, a Hitler, or a Stalin.

---

[1] A summary of the survey appeared in the *San Francisco Chronicle*, November 15, 1969.

[2] Leonard M. Harris, *Long to Reign Over Us?*, p. 144.

³ *Ibid.,* p. 27 and passim.

⁴ Extracts from the address appear in the *Times,* November 10, 1969.

⁵ *New Statesman,* November 14, 1969.

⁶ *Spectator,* November 15, 1969.

⁷ See pp. 170–98 of Andrew Duncan, *The Reality of Monarchy,* for a convenient summary of royal finance. Other essays on the subject are Kingsley Martin, *The Crown and the Establishemnt,* chapter 7; William Hamilton's "The Crown, the Cash and the Future," in Jeremy Murray-Brown, ed., *The Monarchy and its Future*; and Charles Wilcox's "The Finances of the Monarchy," in Lord Altrincham and others, *Is the Monarchy Perfect?*

⁸ In 1760 George III turned over to Parliament for the duration of his reign the revenues from Crown lands in exchange for a fixed income from the Civil List, a practice continued by his successors. In 1969 the revenue from these lands was £3,725,000 and so it is sometimes claimed (for example Charles Petrie, *The Modern British Monarchy,* p. 208) that the nation makes a profit on the monarchy. But as Kingsley Martin observes, it is only "legal fiction" to suggest that these lands still belong to the monarch.

⁹ For recent essays on monarchy see Jeremy Murray-Brown, ed., *The Monarchy and its Future*; Kingsley Martin, *The Crown and the Establishment;* Lord Altrincham and others, *Is the Monarchy Perfect?*; and Drew Middleton, *These Are the British,* chapter 2.

¹⁰ Quoted in Jeremy Murray-Brown, ed., *The Monarchy and its Future,* p. 68.

¹¹ For the Queen as hostess see Dorothy Laird, *How the Queen Reigns,* chapter 10, and Andrew Duncan, *The Reality of Monarchy.* On pp. 352–53 Duncan has a list of those appearing at informal lunches in 1968 and 1969.

¹² *Sunday Telegraph,* June 22, 1969. It should be pointed out that royalty, although at times seeming rather natural and informal, is usually very royal and formal. The Queen is conscious of her position, and allows no one to take liberties.

¹³ For an opposing view see Anthony Sampson, *The Anatomy of Britain Today,* first edition, chapter 2, which is one of the better recent essays on monarchy.

¹⁴ Quoted in John W. Wheeler-Bennett, *King George VI,* p. 820. On the private secretary see John W. Wheeler-Bennett, Appendix B; Kingsley Martin, *The Crown and the Establishment,* Chapter 8; and Helen Hardinge's *Loyal To Three Kings,* which describes the work of Sir Alex Hardinge, private secretary, 1936–1943.

¹⁵ Quoted in John W. Wheeler-Bennett, *King George VI,* pp. 821–22.

¹⁶ D.C. Cooper, "Looking Back on Anger," in Vernon Bogdanor and Robert Skidelsky, editors, *The Age of Affluence, 1951–1964,* p. 260.

¹⁷ *New Statesman,* October 12, 1962.

¹⁸ However, no sovereign would use this power without appropriate consultation with the Prime Minister.

¹⁹ Winston Churchill, *The Gathering Storm,* pp. 10–11. See also Churchill's *Triumph and Tragedy,* pp. 750–53.

²⁰ See Sir Ivone Kirkpatrick, *Mussolini, Study of a Demagogue,* pp. 346–47, and Albert Speer, *Inside the Third Reich,* pp. 55, 110. The Italian and Spanish royal houses made two fatal mistakes: They became associated with one political personality, and they liked to appear politically powerful. An effective parliamentary system has allowed recent British sovereigns to avoid these errors.

²¹ Bernard Brodie, *Strategy In the Missile Age,* p. 134.

THE PSYCHOLOGY OF CONSTITUTIONAL MONARCHY*

ERNEST JONES

What renders the problem of government so very difficult is man's constantly double attitude towards it, the fact that his attitude is always a mixture of two contradictory sets of wishes. On the one hand, he has very deep motives for wishing to be ruled. Feeling unequal to the task of controlling either his own or his neighbour's impulses, and longing to shift the responsibility for so doing, he demands some authority who shall shoulder the main part of this burden. On the other hand, as soon as the restrictions of authority are felt to be oppressive, he is impelled to protest and clamour for freedom. In an ordered society these two sets of impulses have to be co-ordinated, though in a constantly fluctuating rather than in any static form. At times either set may become predominant. When a people's sense of helplessness, inferiority arising from guiltiness, becomes unbearable, there arises a passionate clamour for a "strong" dictatorial government, whether of the autocratic or socialistic variety; while, when a thwarting of personal initiative is felt to be intolerable, there is a call for revolution which may attain a murderous intensity.

Modern psychology well recognizes that these shifting attitudes in the outer world mirror the constant conflict and instability in man's inner nature, the to and fro surges between the expressing and the restraining of his fundamental impulses. It is noteworthy that each side of the conflict may be depicted in either ignoble or laudatory terms. We may speak of the divine call to freedom, one of the noblest impulses in man's nature, as well as of his tendency to unrestrained and brutal licence. On the other hand, the controlling tendencies may assume the form of sheer persecution and hateful thwarting of life as well as the confident self-control that ranks as one of the highest of our civic virtues or the acceptance of God's will so characteristic of the greatest saints.

---

*First published in *The New Statesman and Nation*, February 1, 1936; later incorporated as chapter XVI in *Essays in Applied Psychoanalysis*, Volume I (London, 1951) by Ernest Jones.

It is also well recognized that this dichotomy of man's nature expresses itself most vividly in the child's relation to his parents—the famous Oedipus complex. In the deeper layers of the mind the attitudes persist in their old child-parent terms, though in consciousness they may have been superseded by more complex ones, such as Herbert Spencer's *Man Versus the State*. No psycho-analyst would hesitate, on coming across the person of a ruler in a dream, to translate "ruler" as "father," and he would at once be interested in the way in which the subject's conscious attitude towards the ruler was being influenced by his underlying attitude towards his father. Mostly one should replace the last words by "the underlying *phantastic* attitude towards his father," remembering that in the child's imagination his father is either far more benevolent or far more cruel than most fathers are—and always more magically powerful and wonderful than any father is. It is the persistence in the unconscious of this element of magic belief that accounts for the recurrent irrationalities in people's attitude towards a government, e.g. that blames it for all misfortunes and imputes to its wickedness the nonappearance of an immediate Utopia.

Growing up signifies that the early sense of dependence on the parent (let me say "father," *tout court*), both real and imaginary, is replaced by a proper independence and self-reliance *without* any need for violent repudiation or destruction; also that the insoluble conflict between affection and parricide is replaced by an attitude of friendliness combined with a preparedness to oppose if need be. And any satisfactory solution of the general problem of government must include, among other things, a corresponding advance in the relations between governing and governed. I hope now to be able to show that, whatever its deficiencies may be, the success of the constitutional monarchy experiment is essentially due to the respects in which this advance has been achieved.

The experiment, or idea, starts with the assumption that, just as princesses cannot be abolished from fairy-tales without starting a riot in the nursery, so it is impossible to abolish the idea of kingship in one form or another from the hearts of men. If people are emotionally starved in this way they invent sugar kings, railroad kings, or magic "bosses." The idea then boldly proposes: let us reserve a king particularly to satisfy the beneficent elements of the mythology in man's ineradicable unconscious that will enable us to deal with the more troublesome elements. This is how it is worked out.

The essential purpose of the device is to prevent the murderous potentialities in the son-father (*i.e.* governed-governing) relation from ever coming to too grim and fierce an expression. To effect this the idea of the ruler is "decomposed," as mythologists call it, into two persons —one untouchable, irremovable and sacrosanct, above even criticism, let alone attack; the other vulnerable in such a degree that sooner or later he will surely be destroyed, *i.e.* expelled from his position of power. The first of these, the king, is the symbolic ruler, one not directly responsible to the people; the second, the prime minister, is the functional ruler, exquisitely responsible. With these precautions a safe outlet is available for the parricidal tendencies; they may come into action (a) in a form that excludes physical vio-

lence, and (b) so long as they respect the taboo. Charles II would appear to
have foreseen the coming arrangement when he wittily warded off the criticism of his epitaph-writing courtier with the words: "I' faith, that's true,
since my words are my own, but my deeds are my ministers'."

In return for the concession made by the populace in mollifying their
parricidal tendencies, the government also, by always being ready to accept
the verdict of an election, renounces the application of physical force.
Under a constitutional monarchy no minister labels a cannon, as Louis
XIV did, *ultima ratio regum*. The important point of this consideration is
that the institution of limited monarchy, so far from being simply a
method of dealing with potentially troublesome monarchs, is really an
index of a highly civilized relation subsisting between rulers and ruled. It
could not survive, or even exist, except in a state that has attained the
highest level of civilization, where reasoned persuasion and amicable consent have displaced force as a method of argument.

When Thiers shallowly thought to define a constitutional monarch completely with the words, *le roi regne mais ne gouverne pas*, he was making a
very considerable mistake. In a very deep sense such a king truly represents the sovereign people. I am not here referring to any personal influence of a particular monarch, such as Mr. Gladstone had in mind when he
said that knowing Queen Victoria's opinion told him the opinion of the
English people. But what of the Members of Parliament, the accredited
spokesmen of the people? They are temporarily so, and they may err. But
when the significant words, *le roi le veult*, have been pronounced, it means
in most cases that a permanent representative of the people agrees that
their sovereign voice has been at least not grossly misinterpreted. The
king is carefully shielded from all personal responsibility and yet he represents the final responsibility —and at critical moments may have to bear it.

An odd instance of the far-reaching influence of this sense of finality
came within my experience some years ago. I was talking to the medical
superintendent of a Canadian asylum in his room when a woman entered
and demanded that her husband, a patient there, be discharged. The doctor, knowing the patient's dangerous tendencies, demurred, and a situation
arose which it would have been quite easy to resolve with ordinary tact-
fulness. To my great astonishment, when the woman went on to say
querulously, "What right have you to keep my husband?" the doctor made
a histrionic gesture and declaimed the words "I do so in the name of the
King!" The woman subsided, though it was not quite clear whether it was
surprise or awe had overcome her at the conjuring up of the supreme imperial authority.

The mysterious identification of king and people just hinted at goes
very far indeed and reaches deep into the unconscious mythology that lies
behind all these complex relationships. A ruler, just as a hero, can strike
the imagination of the world in one of two ways. Either he presents some
feature, or performs some deed, so far beyond the range of average people
as to appear to be a creature belonging to another world. We do not know
if the Spanish were really impressed on being told that their Queen could
not accept a gift of silk stockings because she had no legs; but it is easy to

think of less absurd examples, from the deeds of the Borgias to the impertinences of *Le Roi Soleil*. Einstein has furnished us with a current example of another kind. In the face of such phenomena one gapes with wonder or with horror, but one gapes; one does not understand. Or, on the contrary, he may capture the imagination by presenting to us, as it were on a screen, a magnified and idealized picture of the most homely and familiar attributes. It is here that the child's glorified phantasies of himself and his family find ample satisfaction. When the sophisticated pass cynical comments on the remarkable interest the majority of people take in the minute doings of royalty, and still more in the cardinal events of their births, loves, and deaths, they are often merely denying and repudiating a hidden part of their own nature rather than giving evidence of having understood and transcended it. With the others there is no trace of envy, since the illustrious personages are in their imagination their actual selves, their brother or sister, father or mother. In the august stateliness and ceremonial pomp their secret daydreams are at last gratified, and for a moment they are released from the inevitable sordidness and harassing exigencies of mundane existence. When to this is added the innumerable "homely touches" of royalty, the proof that they are of the same flesh as their subjects, together with signs of personal interest and sympathy with their lot, loyalty is infused with affection. And a constitutional monarch, so guarded from adverse criticism, has to have a pretty bad character before he arouses any. An autocratic monarch may be selfish and cruel, but kindliness and friendliness are the natural appurtenances of a constitutional monarch.

The psychological solution of any antinomy which the experiment of constitutional monarchy represents, is also illustrated in the mode of accession of a new monarch. Is this ruler of his people, at the same time their highest representative, chosen by the people to fulfil his exalted office, or does he reign by virtue of some innate and transcendent excellence resident in him from birth? Do the people express freedom in choice or do they submit to something imposed on them? The Divine Right of kings was definitely ended in this country three centuries ago, but what of the right of birth? Here again a subtle compromise has been found. By virtue of an Act of Parliament, *i.e.* an agreement between people and monarch, the Privy Council, with the aid of various unspecified "prominent Gentlemen of Quality," take it on themselves to announce that a son has succeeded to his father, and their decision is universally acclaimed. It is as near the truth as the people's supposed free choice of their functional ruler, the Prime Minister. In neither case do they actively select a particular individual; what happens is that in certain definite circumstances they *allow* him to become their ruler. Their freedom lies in their reserving the right to reject him whenever he no longer plays the part allotted to him.

We have thus learned how to prevent monarchy from degenerating into tyranny; and we are rapidly learning how to prevent timocracy from degenerating into plutocracy. But we have still to learn how to prevent democracy from degenerating into ochlocracy, or aristocracy into oligarchy.

THE CONSTITUTIONAL POSITION OF THE SOVEREIGN*

HERBERT H. ASQUITH

I propose to deal in this memorandum with the position of a Constitutional Sovereign in relation to the controversies which are likely to arise with regard to the Government of Ireland Bill. In a subsequent paper I will deal (1) with the actual and prospective situation in Ireland in the event of (a) the passing, (b) the rejection of that Bill; and (2) with the possibility and expediency of some middle course.

In the old days, before our present Constitution was completely evolved, the Crown was a real and effective, and often a dominating factor in legislation. Its powers were developed to considerable lengths by such Kings as Henry VIII, and enforced with much suppleness and reserve by Queen Elizabeth; but the Tudor Sovereigns had a keen eye and a responsive pulse to the general opinion of the nation. The Stuarts, who followed, pushed matters to extremes, with the result that Charles I lost his head, and James II his throne. The Revolution put the title to the Throne and its prerogative on a Parliamentary basis, and since a comparatively early date in the reign of Queen Anne, the Sovereign has never attempted to withhold his assent from a Bill which had received Parliamentary sanction.

We have had, since that date, Sovereigns of marked individuality, of great authority, and of strong ideas (often from time to time, opposed to the policy of the Ministry of the day) but none of them—not even George III, Queen Victoria or King Edward VII—have ever dreamt of reviving the ancient veto of the Crown. We have now a well-established tradition of 200 years, that, in the last resort, the occupant of the Throne accepts and acts upon the advice of his Ministers. The Sovereign may have lost something of his personal power and authority, but the Crown has been thereby removed from the storms and vicissitudes of party politics, and the monarchy rests upon a solid foundation which is buttressed both

---

*Found in Roy Jenkins, *Asquith*, pp. 543-545.

by long tradition and by the general conviction that its personal status is an invaluable safeguard for the continuity of our national life.

It follows that the rights and duties of a constitutional Monarch in this country in regard to legislation are confined within determined and strictly circumscribed limits. He is entitled and bound to give his Ministers all relevant information which comes to him; to point out objections which seem to him valid against the course which they advise; to suggest (if he thinks fit) an alternative policy. Such intimations are always received by Ministers with the utmost respect, and considered with more care and deference than if they proceeded from any other quarter. But in the end, the Sovereign always acts upon the advice which Ministers, after full deliberation and (if need be) reconsideration, feel it their duty to offer. They give that advice well knowing that they can, and probably will, be called to account for it by Parliament.

The Sovereign undoubtedly has the power of changing his advisers, but it is relevant to point out that there has been, during the last 130 years, one occasion only on which the King has dismissed the Ministry which still possessed the confidence of the House of Commons. This was in 1834, when William IV (one of the least wise of British monarchs) called upon Lord Melbourne to resign. He took advantage (as we now know) of a hint improvidently given by Lord Melbourne himself, but the proceedings were neither well advised nor fortunate. The dissolution which followed left Sir R. Peel in a minority, and Lord Melbourne and his friends in a few months returned to power, which they held for the next 6 years. The authority of the Crown was disparaged, and Queen Victoria, during her long reign, was careful never to repeat the mistake of her predecessor.

The Parliament Act was not intended in any way to affect, and it is submitted has not affected, the constitutional position of the Sovereign. It deals only with differences between the two Houses. When the two Houses are in agreement (as is always the case when there is a Conservative majority in the House of Commons), the Act is a dead letter. When they differ, it provides that, after a considerable interval, the thrice repeated decision of the Commons shall prevail, without the necessity for a dissolution of Parliament. The possibility of abuse is guarded against by the curtailment of the maximum life of any given House of Commons to five years.

Nothing can be more important, in the best interests of the Crown and of the country, than that a practice, so long established and so well justified by experience, should remain unimpaired. It frees the occupant of the Throne from all personal responsibility for the Acts of the Executive and the legislature. It gives force and meaning to the old maxim that "the King can do no wrong." So long as it prevails, however objectionable particular Acts may be to a large section of his subjects, they cannot hold him in any way accountable, and their loyalty is (or ought to be) wholly unaffected. If, on the other hand, the King were to intervene on one side, or in one case—which he could only do by dismissing Ministers in *de facto* possession of a Parliamentary majority—he would be expected to do the same on another occasion, and perhaps for the other side. Every Act of Parliament of the first order of importance, and only passed after acute controversy, would be regarded as bearing the personal *imprimatur* of the Sovereign. He would, whether he wished it or not, be dragged into the arena of party politics; and at a dissolution following such a dismissal of Ministers as has just been referred to, it is no exaggeration to say that the Crown would become the football of contending factions.

This is a Constitutional catastrophe which it is the duty of every wise statesman to do the utmost in his power to avert.

BRITISH MONARCHS: VICTORIA TO ELIZABETH II

MONARCH	ACCESSION	CORONATION
Victoria	June 20, 1837	June 28, 1838
Edward VII	January 22, 1901	August 9, 1902
George V	May 6, 1910	June 22, 1911
Edward VIII	January 20, 1936	———
George VI	December 11, 1936	May 12, 1937
Elizabeth II	February 6, 1952	June 2, 1953

BRITISH MONARCHS AND THEIR PRIME MINISTERS

VICTORIA'S PRIME MINISTERS	PARTY	TERM OF OFFICE
Viscount Melbourne	Whig	1835–41
Sir Robert Peel	Tory (Conservative)	1841–46
Lord John Russell	Whig	1846–52
Earl of Aberdeen	Whig-Peelite	1852–55
Viscount Palmerston	Whig	1855–58
Earl of Derby	Tory (Conservative)	1858–59
Viscount Palmerston	Whig	1859–65
Earl Russell	Whig	1865–66
Earl of Derby	Tory (Conservative)	1866–68
Benjamin Disraeli	Conservative	1868
William Gladstone	Liberal	1868–74
Benjamin Disraeli	Conservative	1874–80
William Gladstone	Liberal	1880–85
Marquis of Salisbury	Conservative	1885–86
William Gladstone	Liberal	1886
Marquis of Salisbury	Conservative	1886–92
William Gladstone	Liberal	1892–94
Earl of Rosebery	Liberal	1894–95
Marquis of Salisbury	Conservative	1895–1902

EDWARD VII'S PRIME MINISTERS	PARTY	TERM OF OFFICE
Marquis of Salisbury	Conservative	1895–1902
Arthur Balfour	Conservative	1902–5
Sir Henry Campbell-Bannerman	Liberal	1905–8
Herbert Asquith	Liberal	1908–15

GEORGE V'S PRIME MINISTERS	PARTY	TERM OF OFFICE
Herbert Asquith	Liberal	1908–15
Herbert Asquith	Coalition	1915–16
David Lloyd George	Coalition	1916–22
Andrew Bonar Law	Conservative	1922–23
Stanley Baldwin	Conservative	1923–24
Ramsay MacDonald	Labour	1924
Stanley Baldwin	Conservative	1924–29
Ramsay MacDonald	Labour	1929–31
Ramsay MacDonald	National	1931–35
Stanley Baldwin	Conservative (National)	1935–37

EDWARD VIII'S PRIME MINISTER	PARTY	TERM OF OFFICE
Stanley Baldwin	Conservative (National)	1935–37

GEORGE VI'S PRIME MINISTERS	PARTY	TERM OF OFFICE
Stanley Baldwin	Conservative (National)	1935–37
Neville Chamberlain	Conservative (National)	1937–40
Winston Churchill	Coalition	1940–45
Winston Churchill	Conservative	1945
Clement Attlee	Labour	1945–51
Winston Churchill	Conservative	1951–55

ELIZABETH II'S PRIME MINISTERS	PARTY	TERM OF OFFICE
Winston Churchill	Conservative	1951–55
Sir Anthony Eden	Conservative	1955–57
Harold Macmillan	Conservative	1957–63
Sir Alec Douglas-Home	Conservative	1963–64
Harold Wilson	Labour	1964–70
Edward Heath	Conservative	1970–

THE ROYAL FAMILIES OF EUROPE

1.

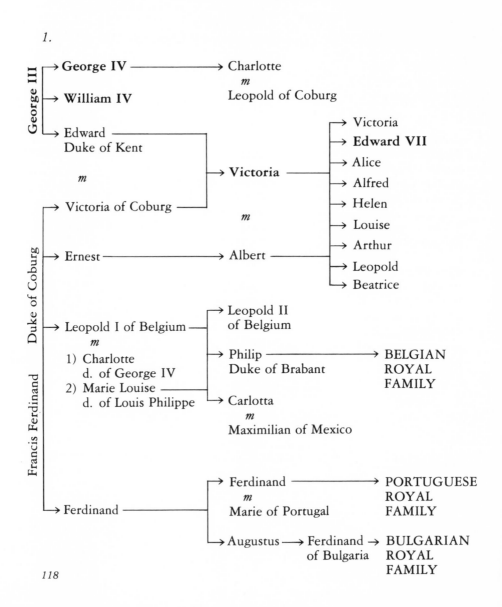

2.

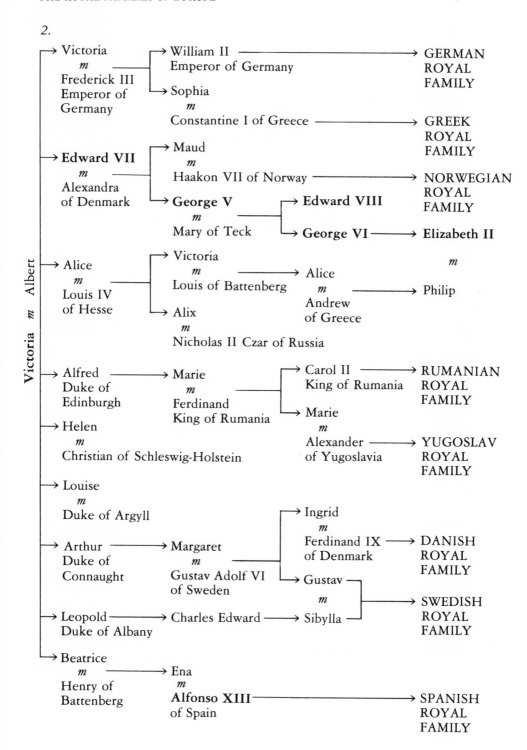